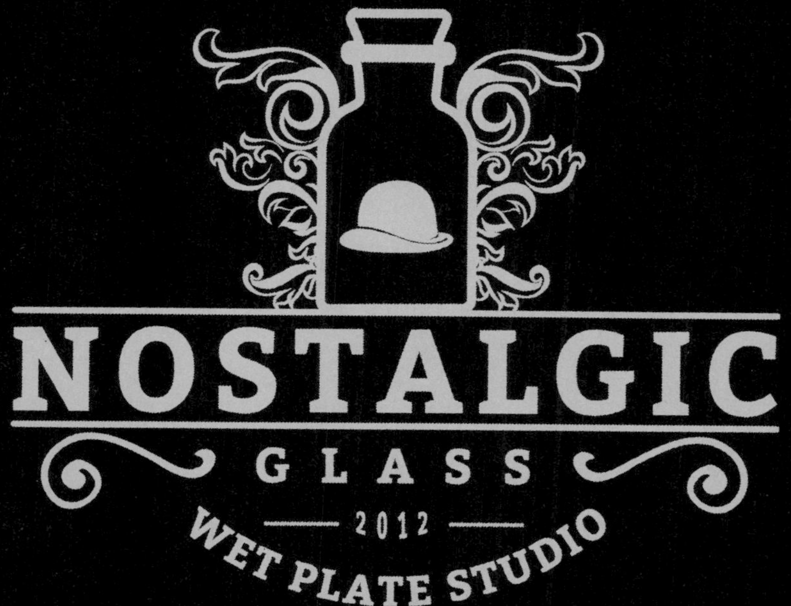

Shane B. Balkowitsch
Ambrotypist

This is number 524 of 2000 limited editions of this book.

Northern Plains Native Americans

A Modern Wet Plate Perspective

Shane Balkowitsch Ambrotypist

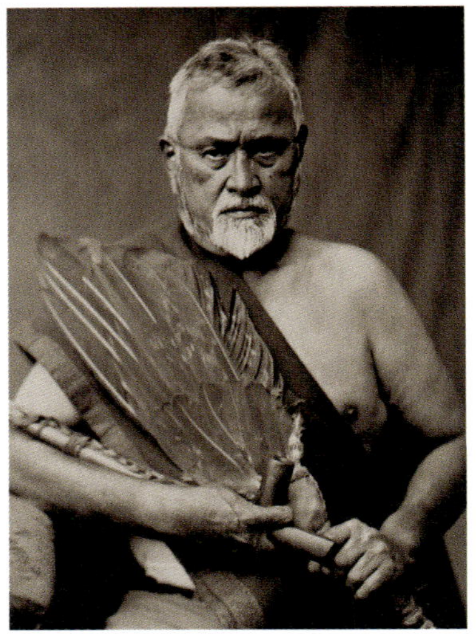

At the end of our Creation story One Man said, "I will make people resembling me and I will give them ceremonies; and you," he said to the buffalo bull, "shall stay with them and shall be their leader." For this reason, we must have a buffalo skull in every ceremony. This is why I have a buffalo skull in this portrait of myself; to honor those who have come before me.

I wear my Red Blanket as a member of the Eagle Sun Dance, which is also why I have an Eagle Wing fan. Eagles figured prominently in my spiritual life; from being a member of the Water Buster clan whose grandfathers are two Eagles that became humans whose skulls we still honor to my 12-year participation in the Eagle Sun Dance.

The pipe I am holding is a large black ceremonial pipe dedicated to the Thunder Birds, who are the grandfathers of eagles. The butte on which I fasted many times is named Thunder Nest butte, said to be the home of Thunder birds. For these reasons, I have the right to give the name Shadow Catcher to my friend and benefactor Shane Balkowitsch. What he has done with these portraits will be remembered for generations, just like Edward S. Curtis and George Catlin.

September 15th, 2023
Calvin Grinnell "Running Elk"
Mandan Hidatsa Arikara Nation

First edition, 2024

Library of Congress Cataloging-in-Publication data is available from the publisher.

Hardcover edition
ISBN: 978-1-943876-63-1
Printed and bound in Latvia

Graphic Design and Layout by Chelsy Ciavarella
Proofreading by Emily Kubischta

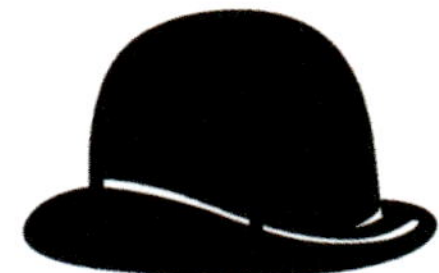

Published in 2024 by
Shane Balkowitsch
Nostalgic Glass Wet Plate Studio
2703 Big Sky Circle
Bismarck, ND 58503

shane@balkowitsch.com
www.nostalgicglasswetplatestudio.com

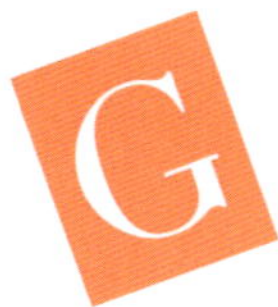

Distributed by
G Editions
500 Seventh Avenue
8th Floor
New York, NY 10018

www.geditions.com
media@geditions.com

Contents

Proceeds from the sale of this book will benefit the American Indian College Fund.
Only 14% of Native Americans have a bachelor's degree and it is an honor to be able to raise funds for this important cause.

https://collegefund.org/

Foreword

Capturing Time

author of The Last Ghost Dancer

Tony Jon Bender

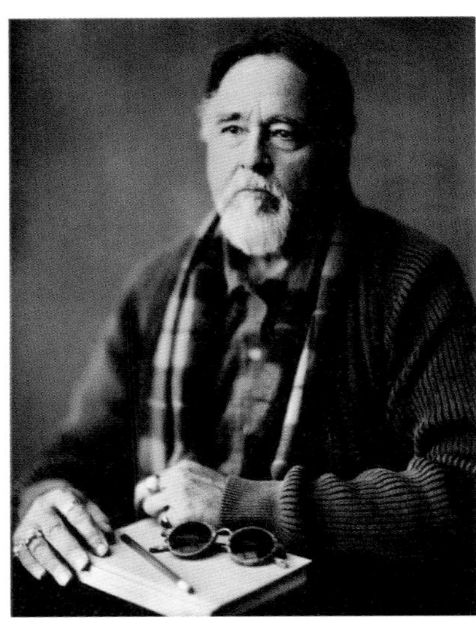

"I imagine Shane as a master of time. That in those 8 to 10 seconds when the lens cover is removed and all breath ceases, he's capturing the soul of his subject."

Poets, philosophers, and scientists have tried to explain it. Time. Is it linear? One point to another into infinity? A beginning we can't fathom into the never ending. That's how we experience it. Or imagine it.

We bear witness to this: emergence we can't recall, but those we love assure us that it happened. Terminus that's almost always a surprise. Eyes wide open. Or closed. Conscious. Or unaware. No one knows for sure what happens. The experts have vanished. The discovery is ours.

Perhaps endings and beginnings are an illusion. Perhaps all is continuance. All is all. And echoes are forever.

When I consider Shane Balkowitsch's timeless art, I think about these things. Before photography, the great masters seemed to capture the soul of their subjects with a brush. It's what set them apart. That's what sets Shane apart.

First, the vision, sizing up the subject. Accoutrements tell a story, too. Like the cover of a book, the purpose is to lure the art into your hands, before your eyes. But it's what's inside that matters. Any cell phone accident can capture a moment. Shane captures souls, and I think, time itself.

Maa'ishda tehxixi Agu'agshi, the Hidatsa call him—Shadow Catcher.

Shadow Catcher. It sounds somewhat dreary until you remember that shadows cannot exist without the light. Yin. Yang. Balance.

Time. Perhaps it's circular, like the hands of a clock, a treadmill. Endless steps forward. Yet, stationary. But there has to be progress; it would be too cruel if there wasn't a point to it all. Birth. Rebirth. Evolution. Karma. A destination. This can't be some accidental agnostic machine propped up by the poets, can it? Surely there is a purpose.

Then there's this theory... time is now. Always. Everything. Everything in an instant. No beginning. No end. No past. No future. Just now. Absolute destinies coexist with zillions of possibilities, dimensions stacked forever high. Then is now. Tomorrow is now.

That's the concept.

A revelation of the mystics, probably ... some ancient sage, alone in a cave divining the universe, an attainer of enlightenment, but what good is that if you don't experience life? Live it. Learn from it. Make mistakes. Evolve. And if you don't take the chance is it really enlightenment?

" Shadow Catcher. It sounds somewhat dreary until you remember that shadows cannot exist without the light. "

Explore.

So many questions. So little time, you say. Well, it depends upon the theory to which you ascribe.

Einstein, who like Cayce, must have channeled the omnipresence, suggested that time is malleable, that a rocket man could travel at light speed, away and back, and find that all he knew had been replaced. Or maybe it was there, dimensionally, all along.

Others, inebriated back-alley savants, perhaps, say you are your own universe, and that this, and all those around you, are your invention. Well, hello, God! And good on you for imagining Shane Balkowitsch. Or thanks, Shane, for imagining us.

I imagine Shane as a master of time. That in those 8 to 10 seconds when the lens cover is removed and all breath ceases, he's capturing the soul of his subject. And that is why the portraits in this book speak to you.

This is different from instant photography that might capture a football in mid-flight, a basketball suspended in the net. Microscopics. Molecules colliding. That's the necessary science of imprints and stains.

This is art. You can learn science. And relearn it when new facts and theories come along. But artists are born. We're an artistic species, but not everyone discovers their destiny in this lifetime. Eventually, they will. Shane has.

We need artists and the museums that house such works because when all seems lost, we're able to visit these shrines and be reminded of the beauty of which mankind is capable. That there's hope for our suicidal genus.

This is sacred work. What Shane is doing is reconnecting indigenous generations, binding together the past and the now. Reminding us, relatives all, of the enduring wisdom, beauty, awareness, and interconnectedness necessary for our survival. Our evolution.

These cultures have much to teach. We all have much to learn. Here is the window. Look.

May it inspire your journey.

They are, in my opinion, a part of the healing.

Shane Balkowitsch

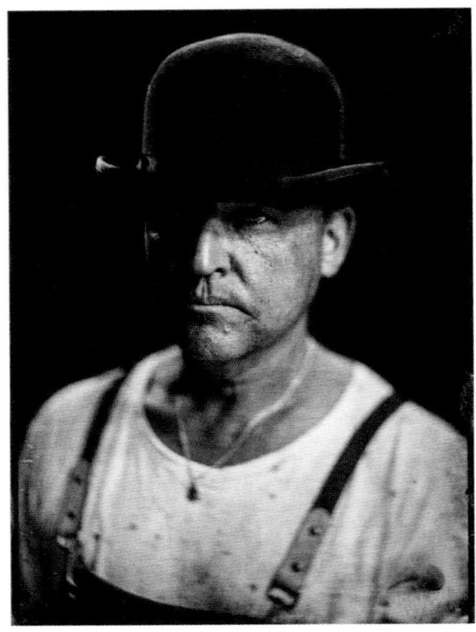

Photo Credit: Joseph W. Brown

It is hard to believe that I am now three fourths of the way to my goal of 1000 portraits for this series. When I first started on this path the task was to take ten portraits of Native Americans. It soon became 50, then 100 and after much contemplation I decided on 1000. Knowing very well that this would take me between ten to fifteen years to achieve. It seemed like an impossible goal at the time.

I recently received another tour of the vault at the State Historical Society of North Dakota at the Heritage Center. This tour was extra special for me because Emily Kubischta was present. She is the first person at the state archive to identify my work as historically significant. She was instrumental in getting my first plate into the archive. That plate was of Ernie LaPointe the Great Grandson of Sitting Bull. Ernie was given the honor of naming the plate and his response was "Eternal Field". This would become ground zero, plate #1, for the series and all other Native portraits would follow.

As I type this, the State Historical Society has curated over 900 of my plates. To see them all sitting there neatly organized, indexed, labeled and protected on the shelves brought a tear to my eye. It seems that I have had my head down for so long working diligently one plate at a time that I was unaware of the scale of the series itself. I knew at that very moment if fate does not break my stride, we will see the completion of the series.

I have been asked about how I select the cover for each volume. It was obvious to me that the portrait of Ernie should have the honor for Volume One. For Volume Two I felt it was crucial to have a female represented and Kristen Joy Tootoosis was given the honor. For this volume it seemed obvious to include youth and the future of the culture. Redsky Starr was perfect for that role. Every time I made a portrait that would become the cover, it became immediately obvious to me what I had. This I cannot explain.

Another question that I field is why I am including images outside of the Northern plains. When the series was first conceptualized it needed a formal name. With the help of the Historical Society we decided on "Northern Plains Native Americans: A Modern Wet Plate Perspective". There would have been no way we would have known that the series would expand outside of our local area. So as the series gained momentum, indigenous people started traveling in from all over the country and in some cases from outside the United States. Even though the scope of the series has reached further than the Northern plains tribes, it is important to keep the original name for consistency. I have thought about changing the name on several occasions but I like the fact that it has remained the same and should remain the same no matter where this takes us. There has always been one rule, no indigenous person will ever be turned down if they want to participate. There simply is no barrier to enter.

Introduction

The Visible Truth

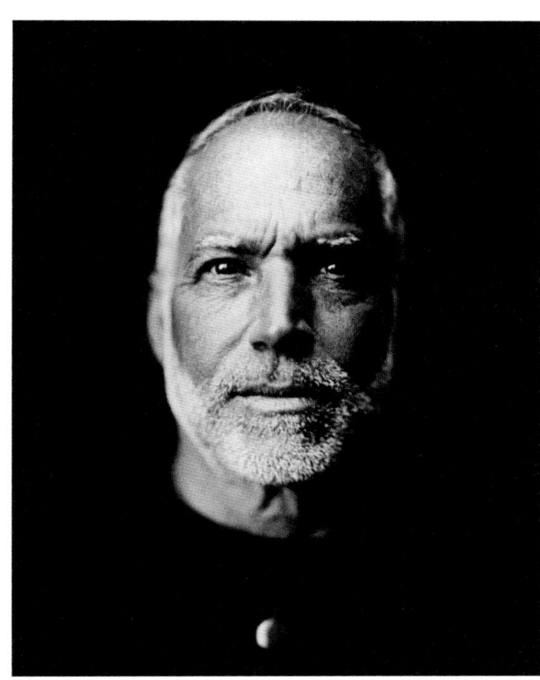

I went to a place where the future and past meet and become intertwined. Where everyone you've ever been comes face to face with who you always hoped to be. Where your prior self passes forward some message or piece of information your future self will need.

It was as if I was taking part in an archaeological dig. The outcome, I discovered, the visible truth; the message for future me would be commensurate with the amount of access I granted to the lens; Shane's lens.

I'm aware we're talking about a photograph, but these are not just any photographs. In our harried, modern world, consumed with speed and efficiency, these ten-second exposures become portals through which we glimpse an alternate universe.

Shane's photographs capture the delicate nuance of breath, the faint heartbeat of a thought, and the essence of a soul laid bare; reveal entire lives and tell stories that are profound. They are unspoken and need no interpretation or explanation.

They are connections. They are relationships. They are trust. They are love.

Look for me in the eyes.
Feel the warmth of my breath.
Think my thoughts.
And when I am gone,
See yourself in the pane of glass.

October 21st, 2023
Chris DiCroce

Nostalgic Glass Natural Light Studio

Bismarck, North Dakota

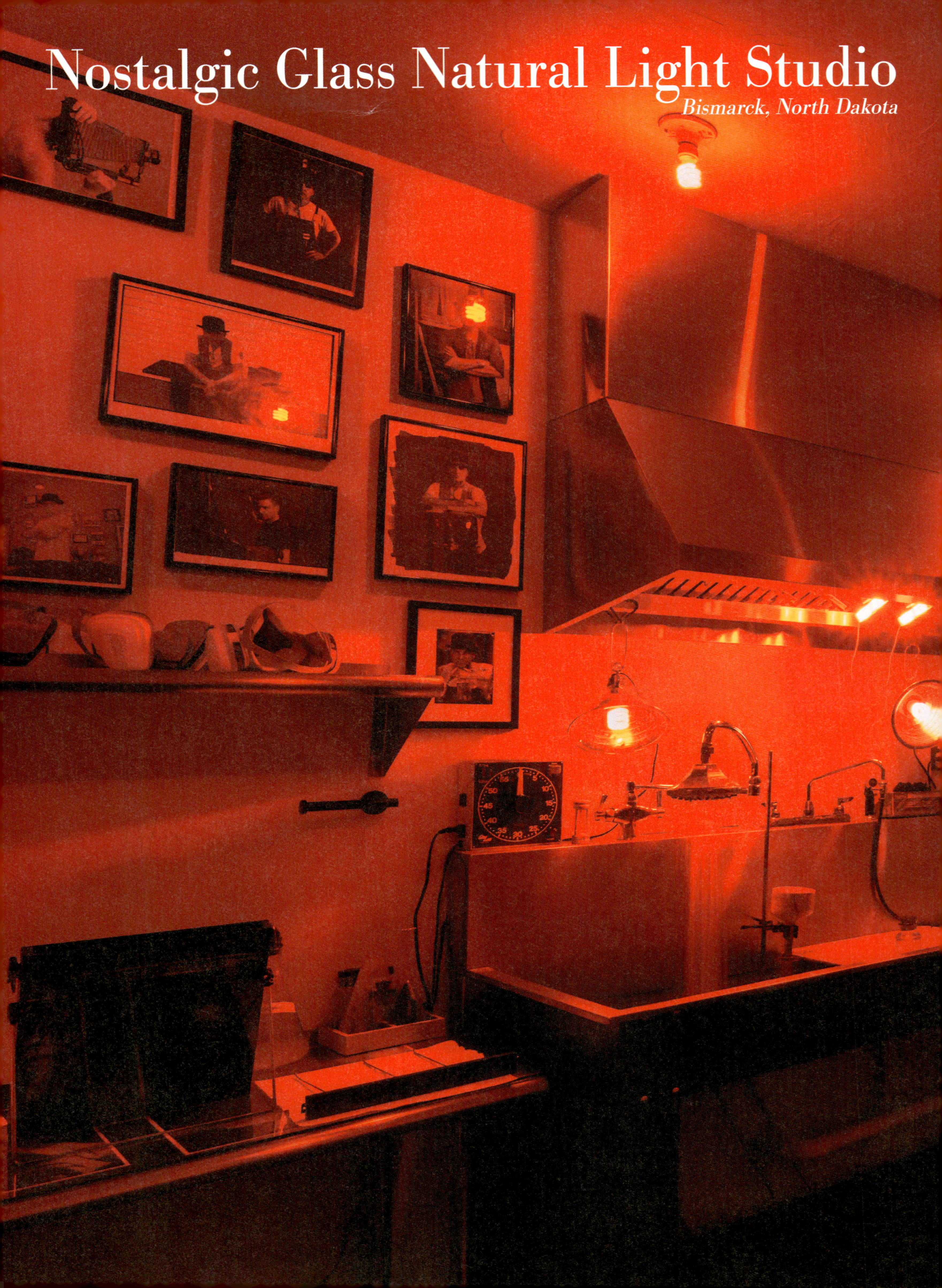

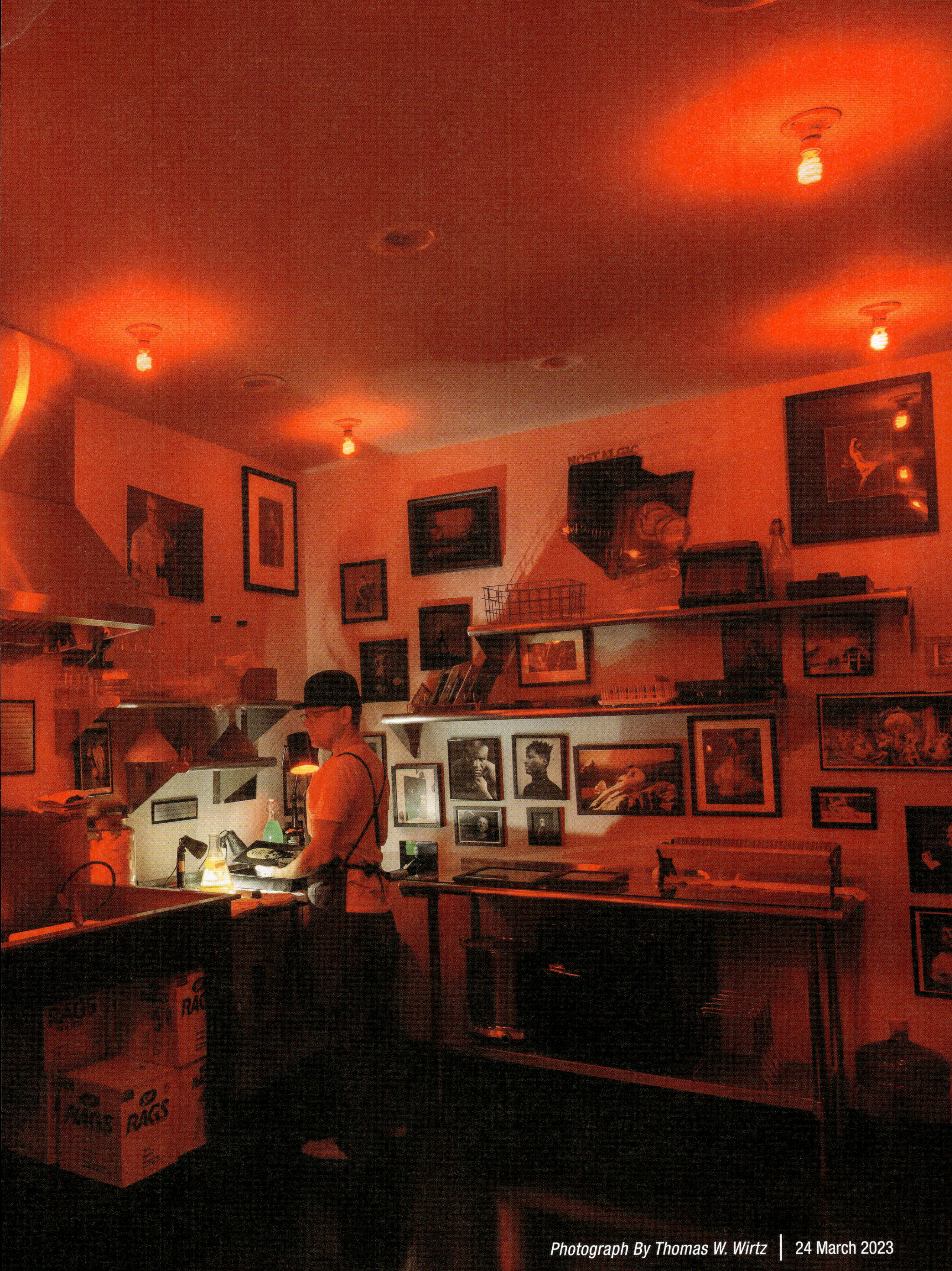

Photograph By Thomas W. Wirtz | 24 March 2023

"Warm Mist" *Azelena Jozett Rosales* | Turtle Mountain Ojibwe / Cora | 29 September 2023 | Plate No. 4820

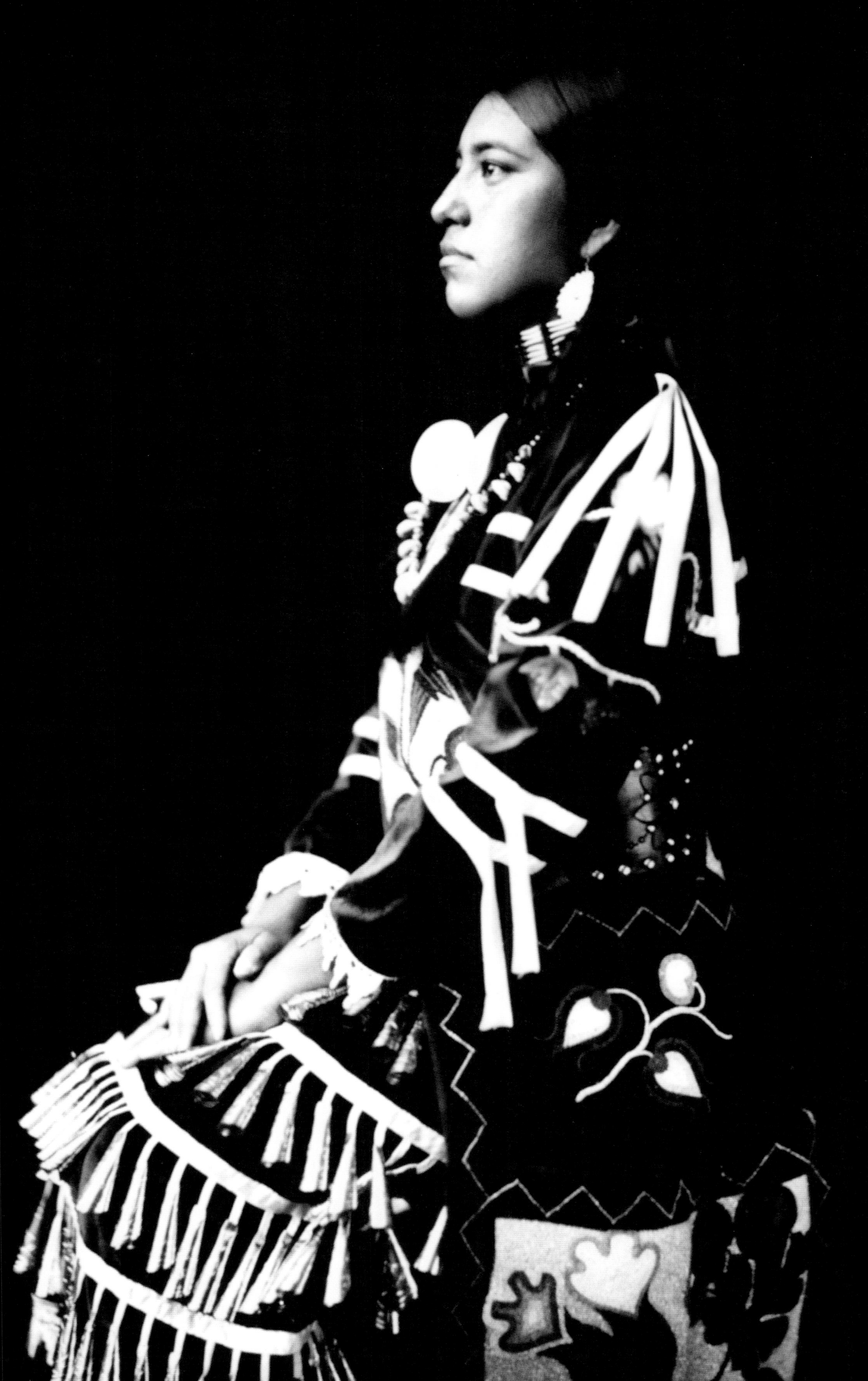

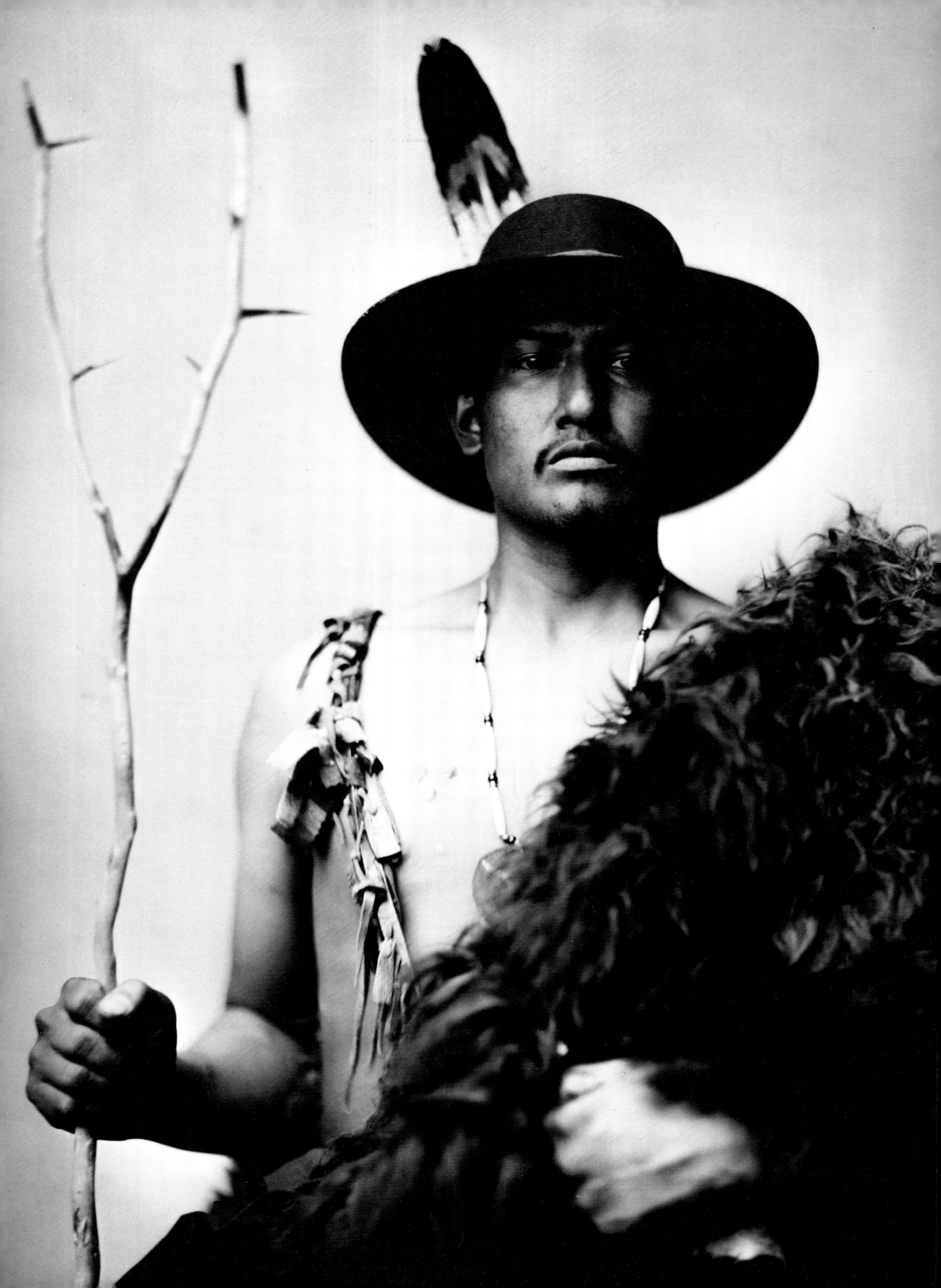

"Black Spotted Horse" *Black Spotted Horse* | Hunkpapa | 13 May 2022 | Plate No. 4250

"Rolling Thunder" *Denver Bryce Spotted Bear* | Mandan / Hidatsa / Arikara | 28 January 2022 | Plate No. 4137

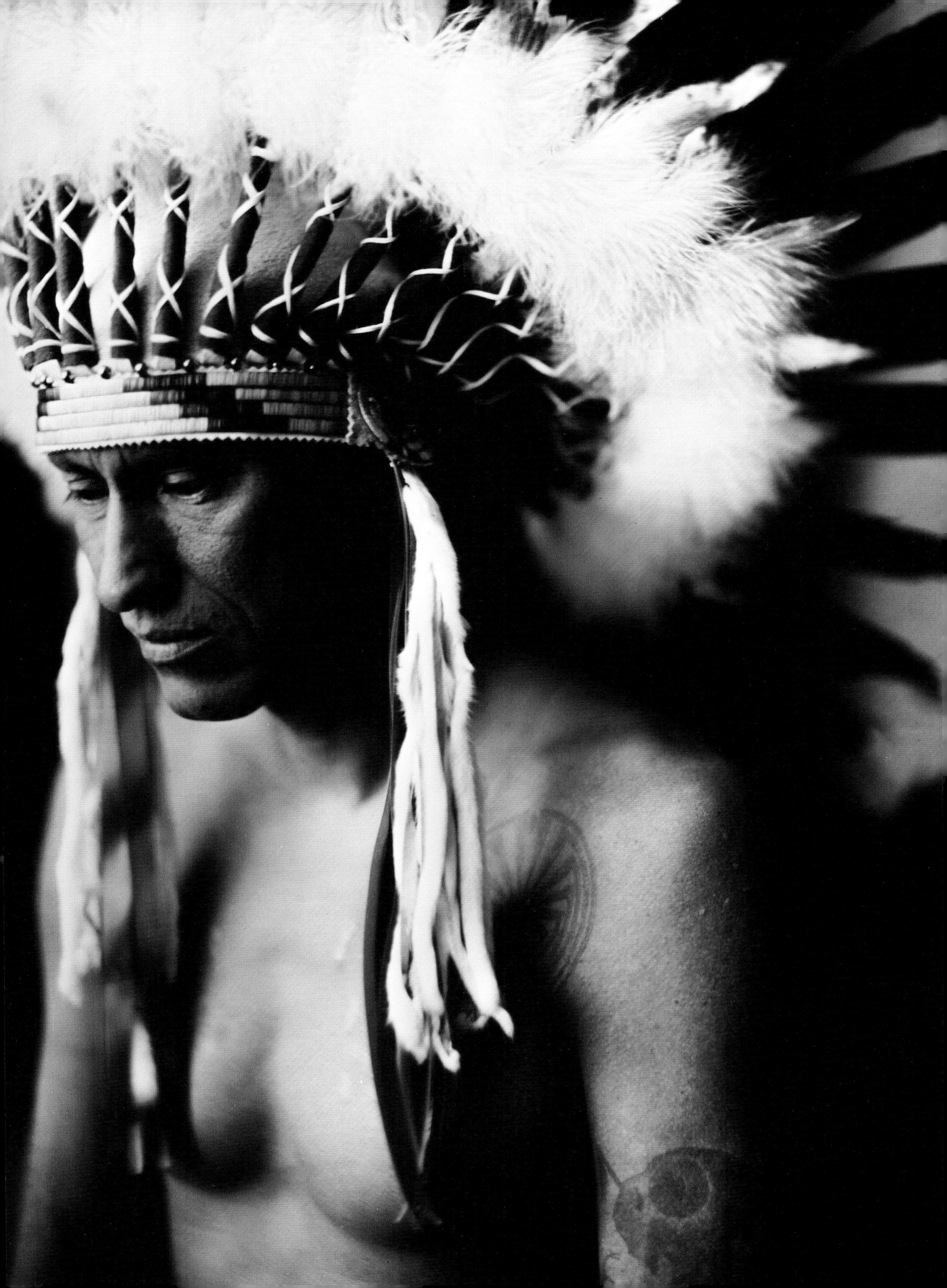

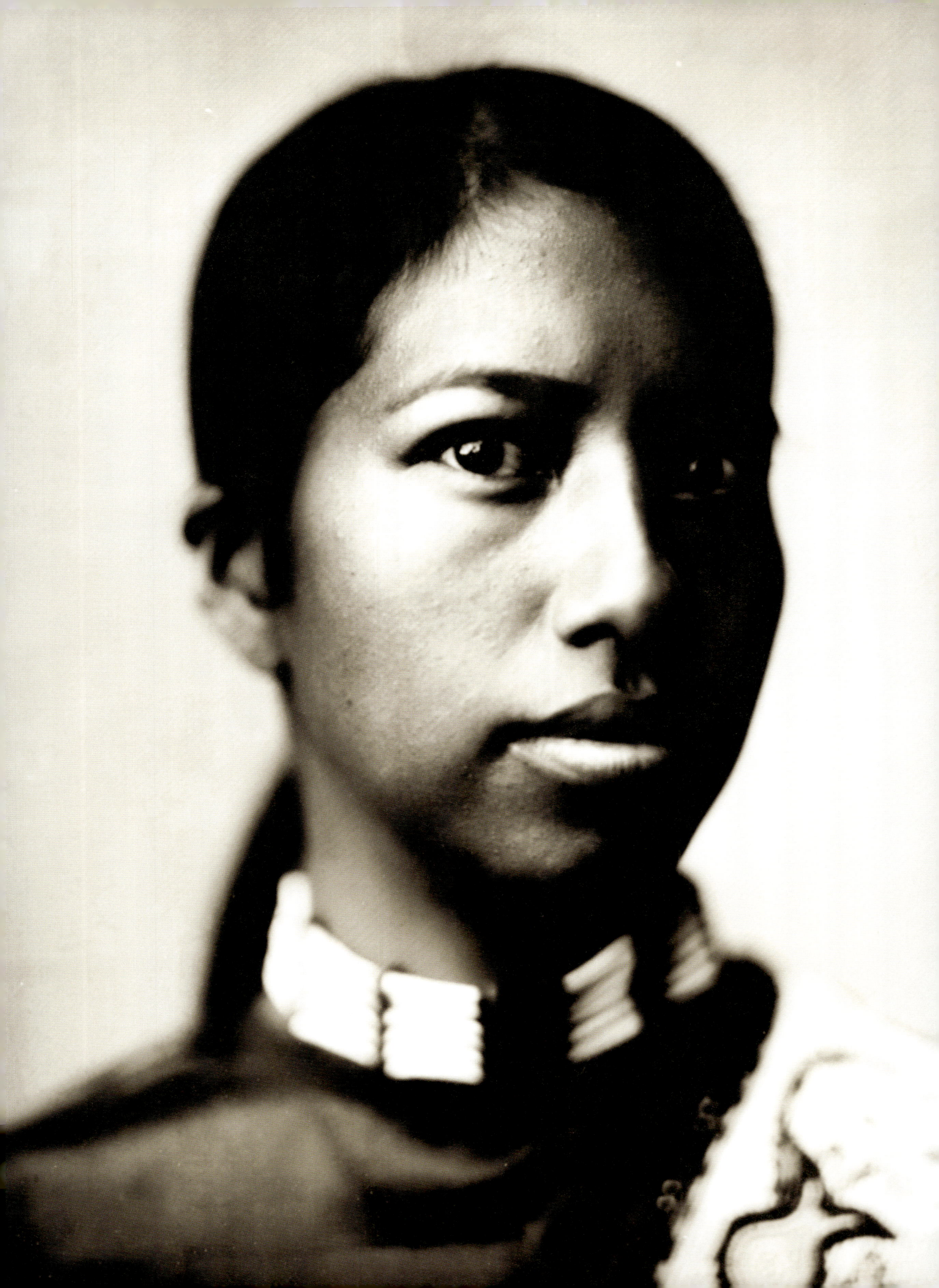

"Shining Star From The West" *Genesis Elisa Rosales* | Turtle Mountain Ojibwe / Cora | 29 September 2023 | Plate No. 4821

"Two Spirit" *Gregory Seth LeBeau* | Turtle Mountain Band of Chippewa / Cheyenne River Lakota Sioux | 1 April 2022 | Plate No. 4214

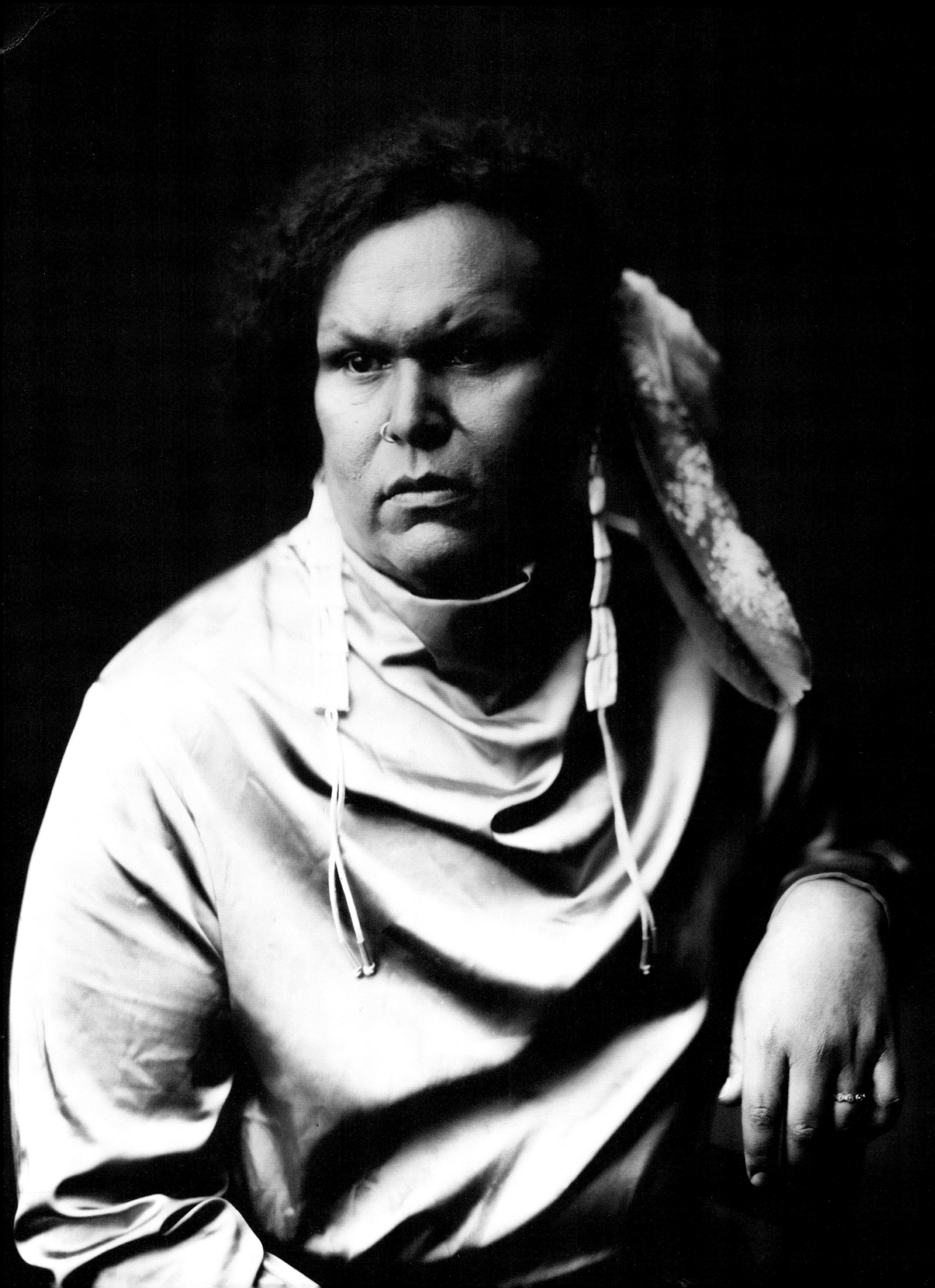

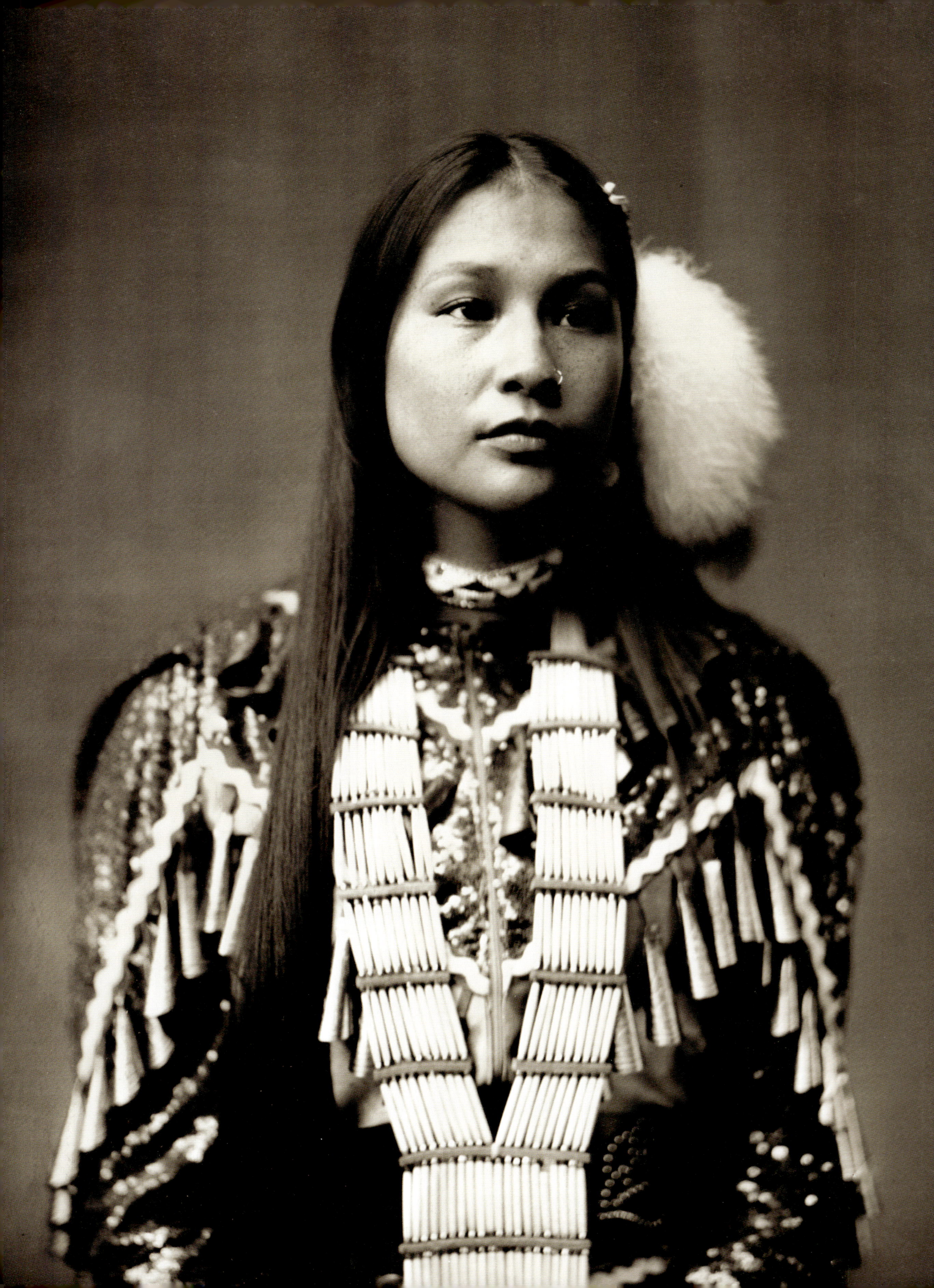

"Thunderbird Woman Calling From Afar" *Cree Rayah Sage Delorme* | Cree / Ojibwe / Dakota | 2 June 2023 | Plate No. 4682

“Taylor” *Dayla Alea Taylor* | Isanti Dakota | 9 December 2022 | Plate No. 4501

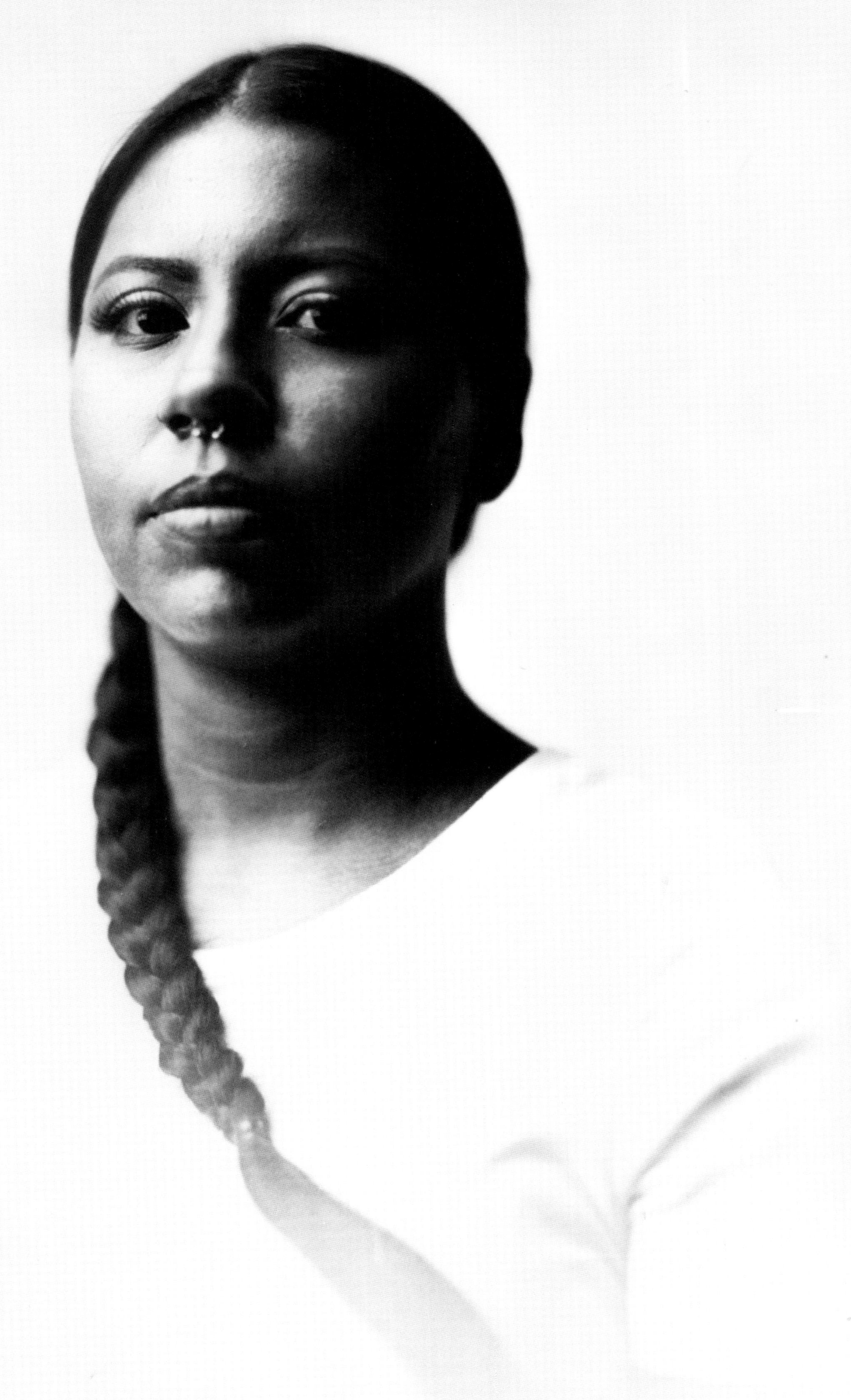

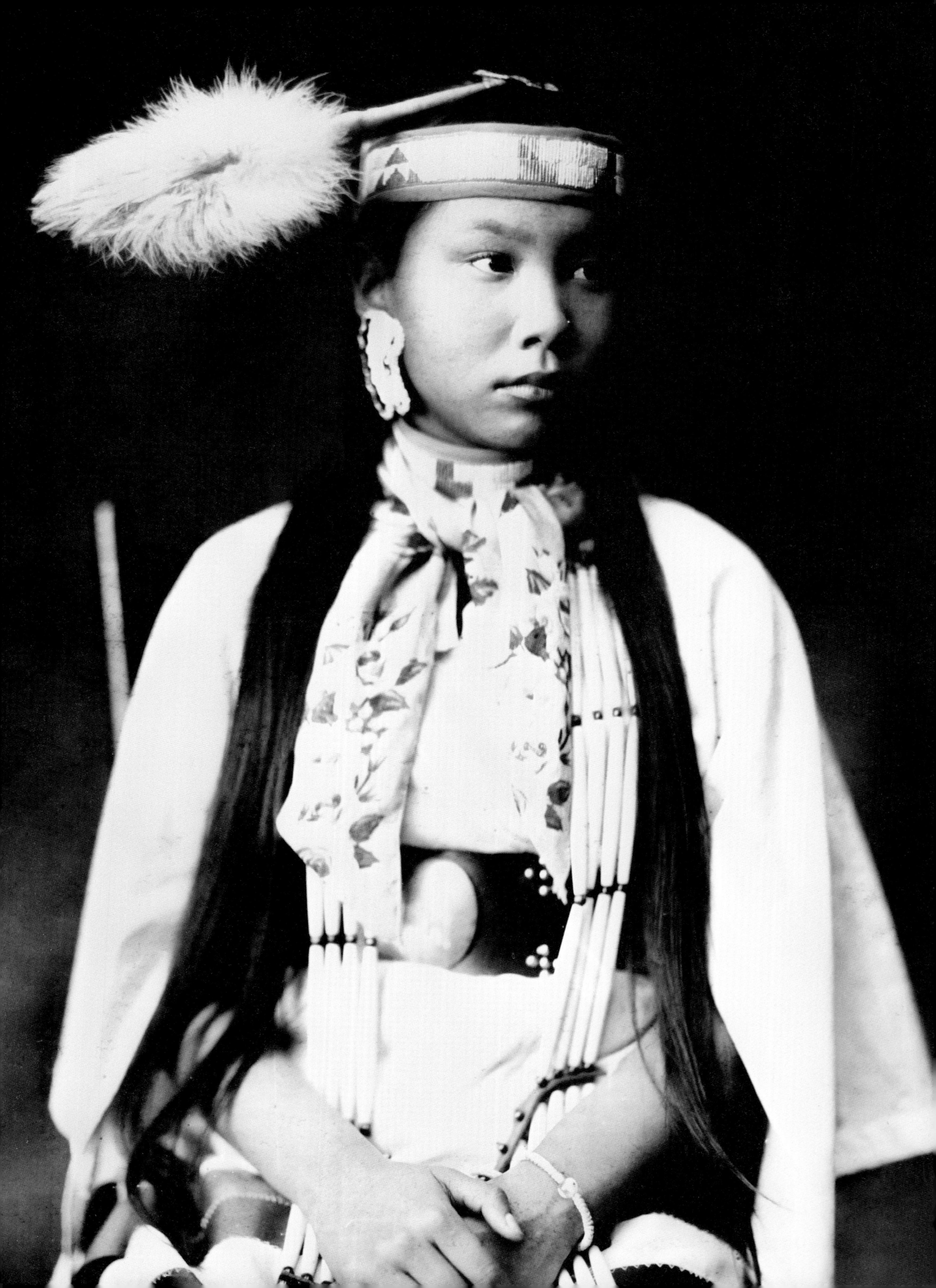

"Yellow Buffalo Woman" *Audrey Carmen Rayn Abdo* | Yankton Sioux / Rosebud Sioux / Santee Sioux | 22 January 2023 | Plate No. 4531

"St. John" *James Elden St. John* | Crow Creek Hunkpati Dakota | 8 September 2023 | Plate No. 4785

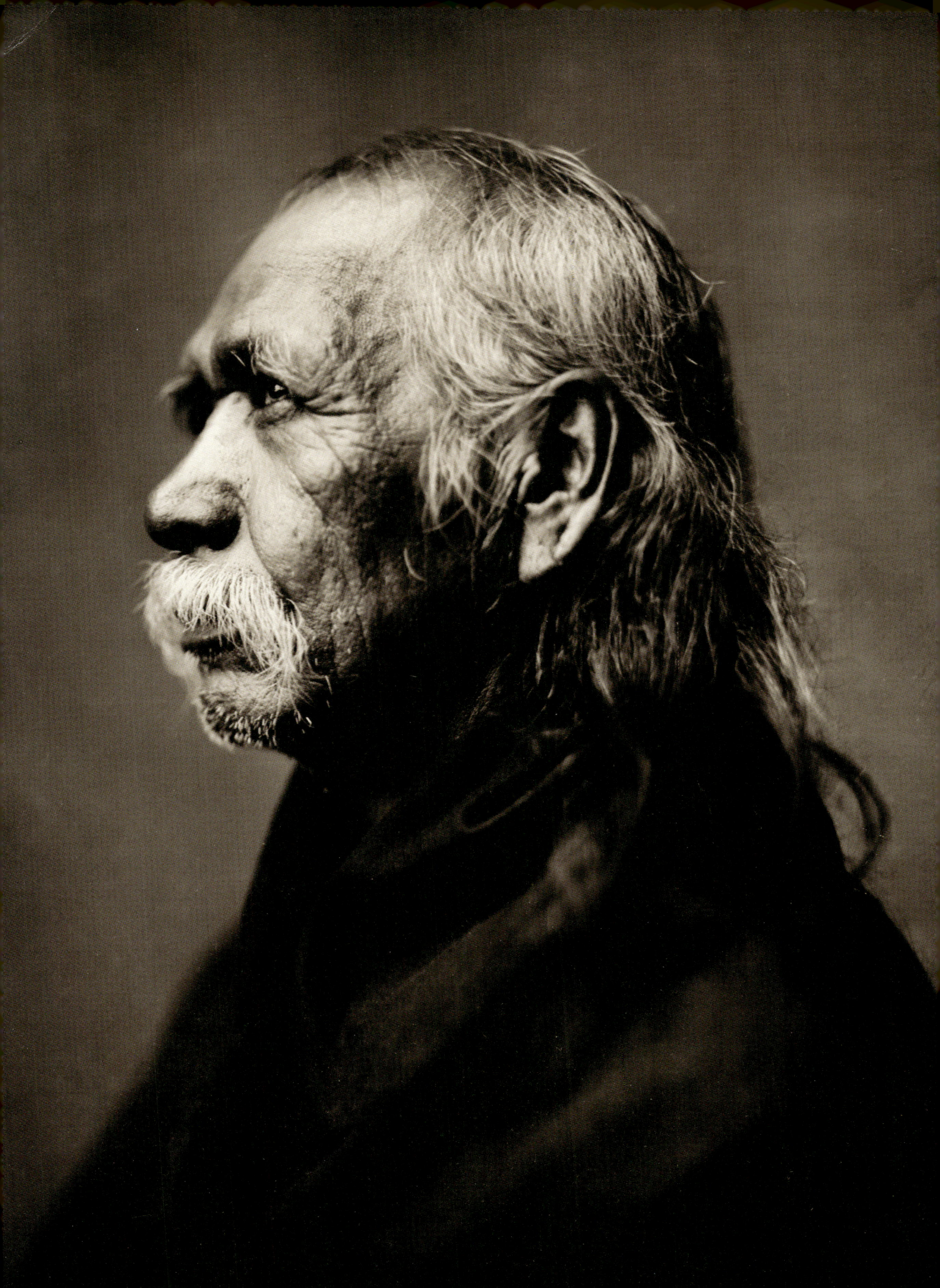

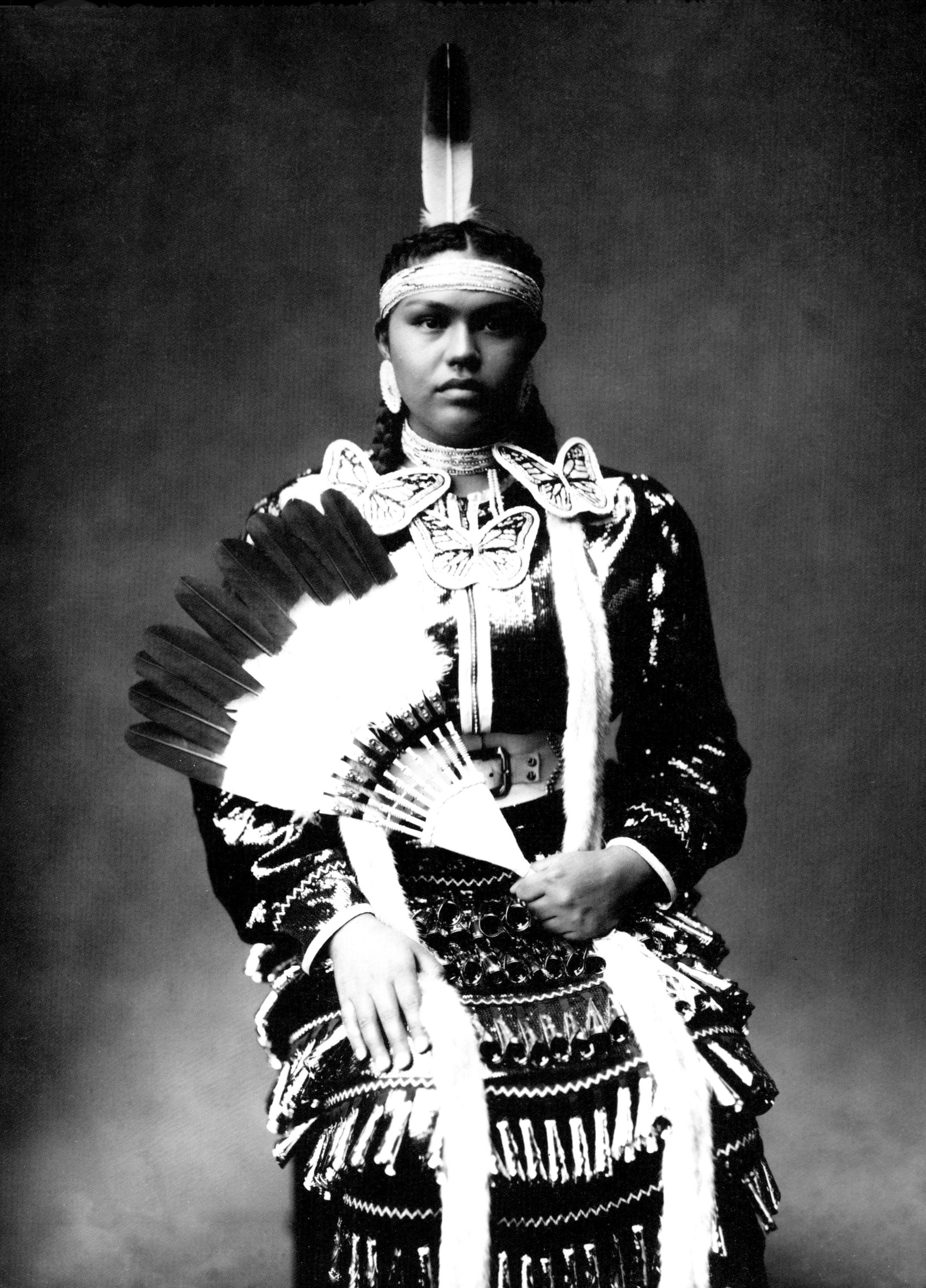

"Bruno" *Kiya Kay-Lynn Bruno* | Cree First Nation from Samson Cree Nation | 1 July 2022 | Plate No. 4304

"Talking Raven" *Corey Lee Davis, Jr.* | Hunkpapa Sioux / Turtle Mountain Band of Chippewa | 20 May 2022 | Plate No. 4266

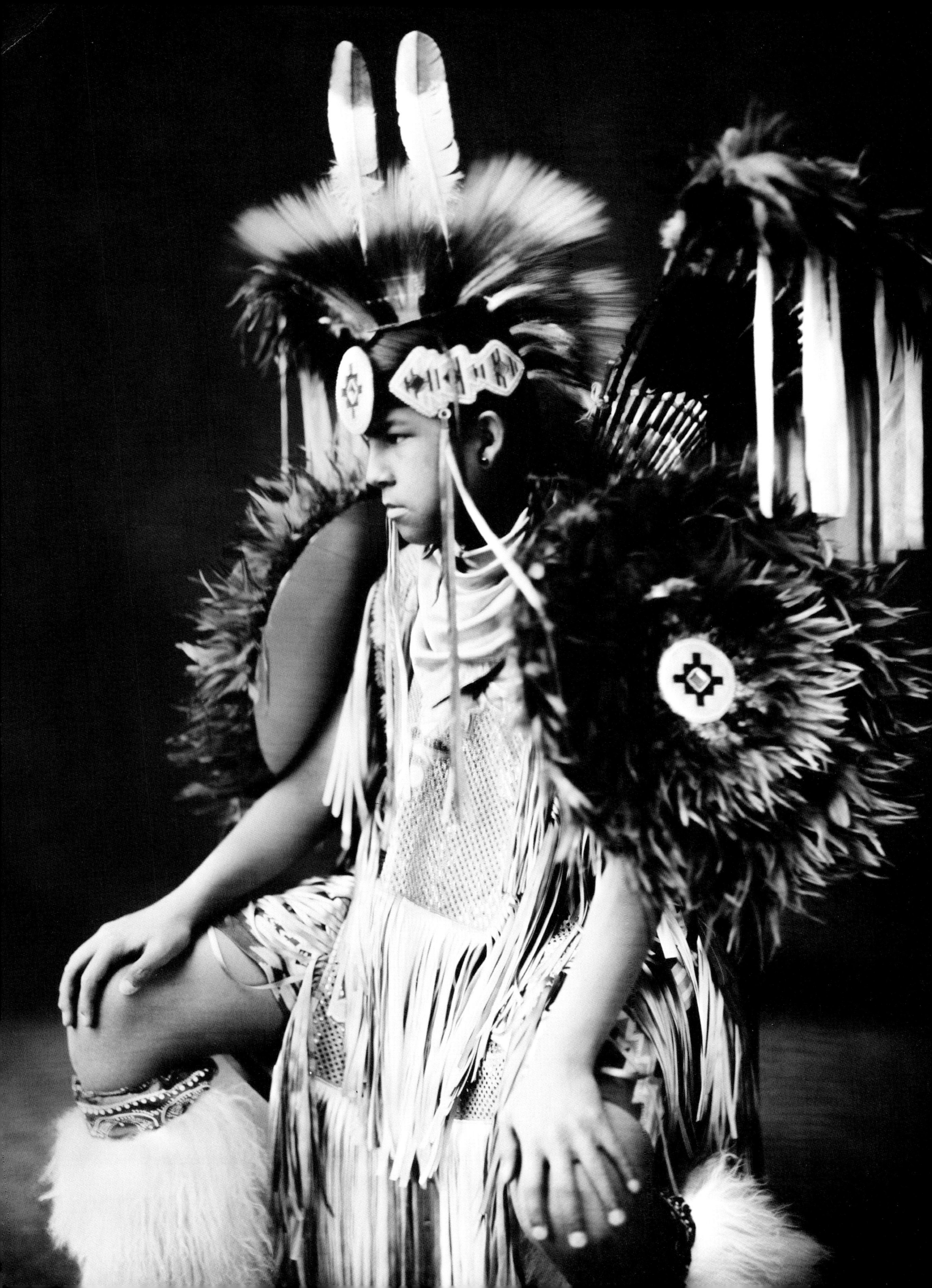

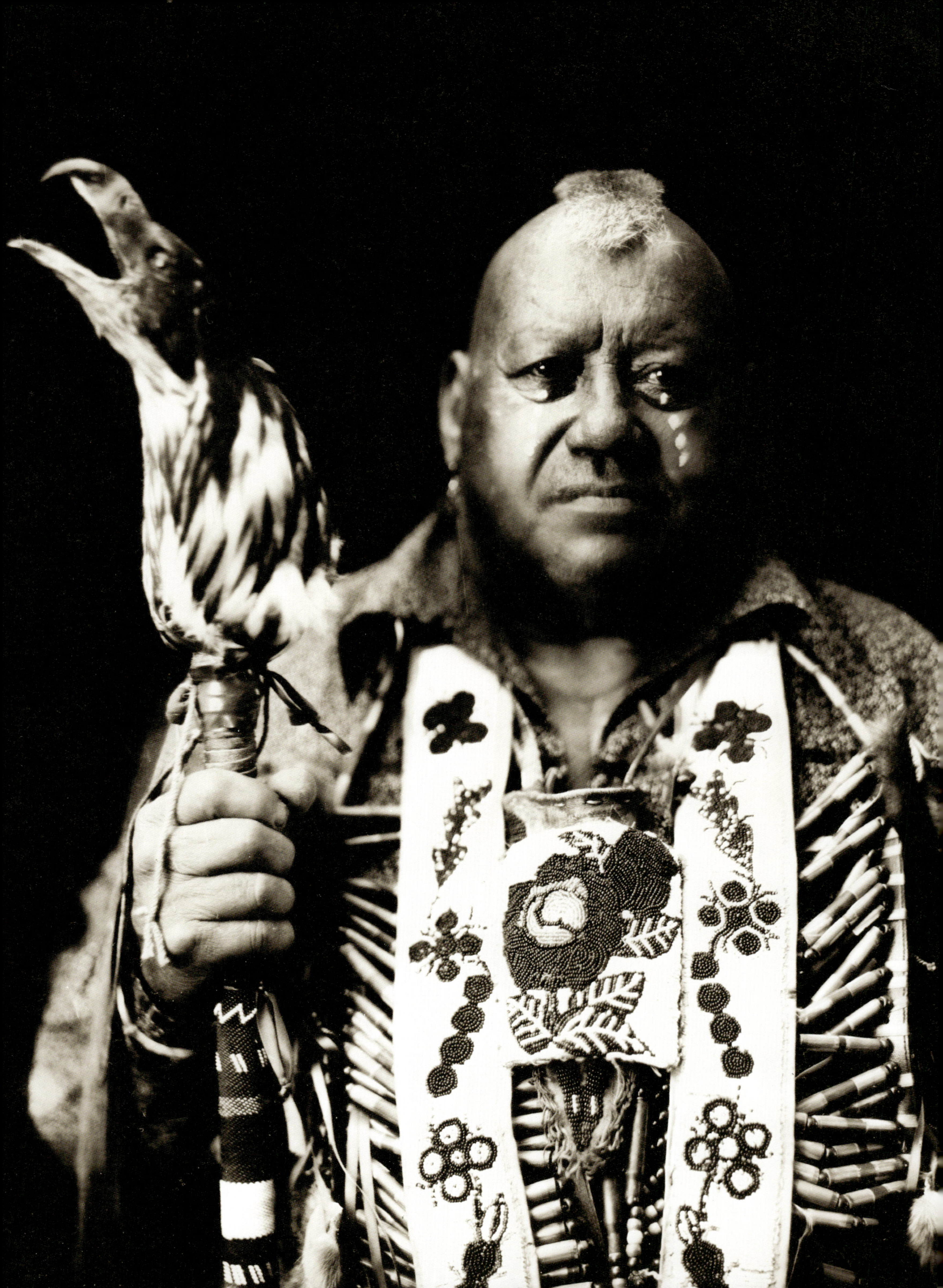

"Holy Man" *Duane Romaine McGillis* | Turtle Mountain Band of Chippewa | 3 March 2023 | Plate No. 4574

"Bear Turns Itself Around And Makes Them Well" *Gerald Anthony Jefferson* | Hidatsa / Hunkpapa | 2 September 2022 | Plate No. 4376

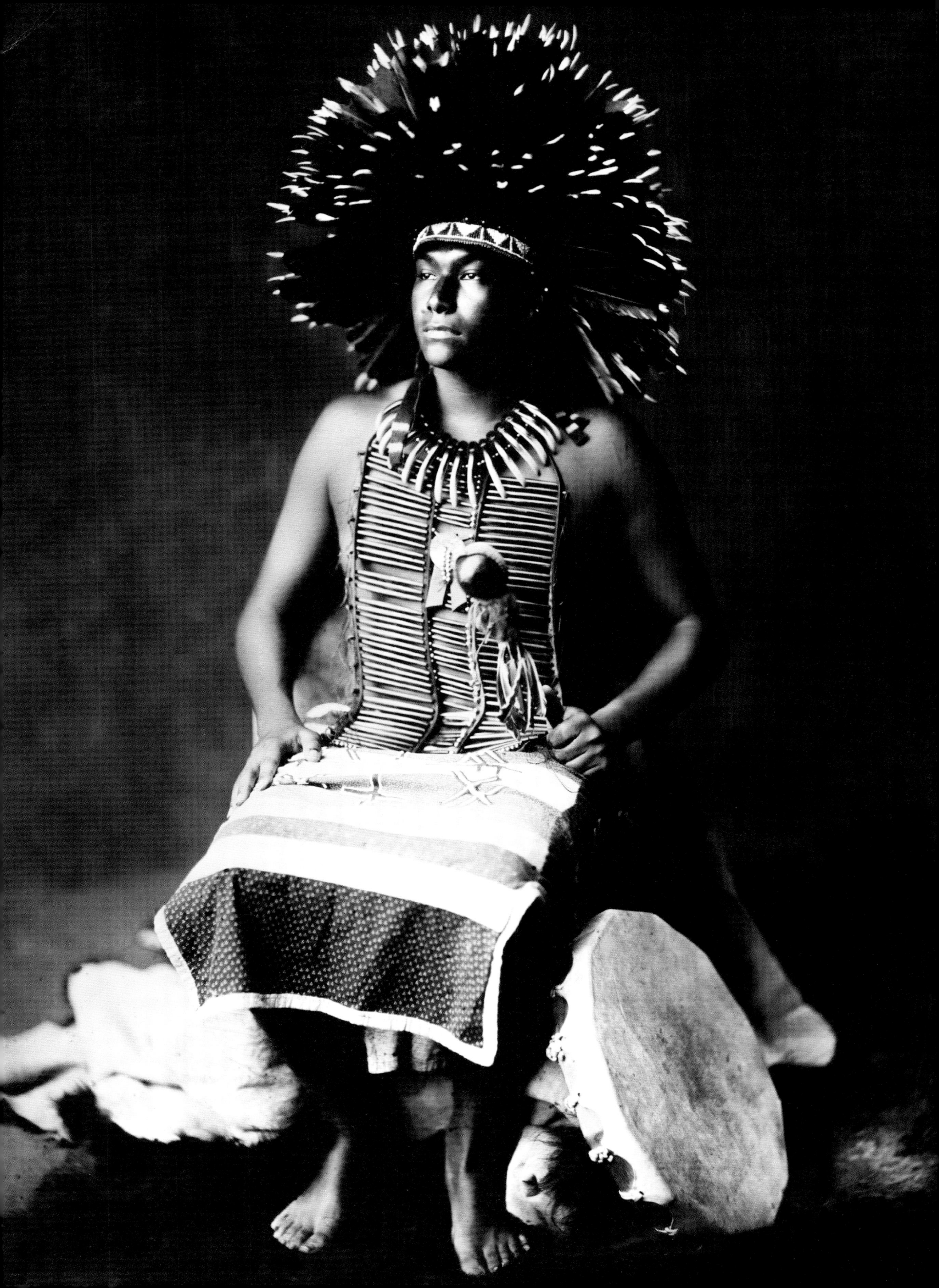

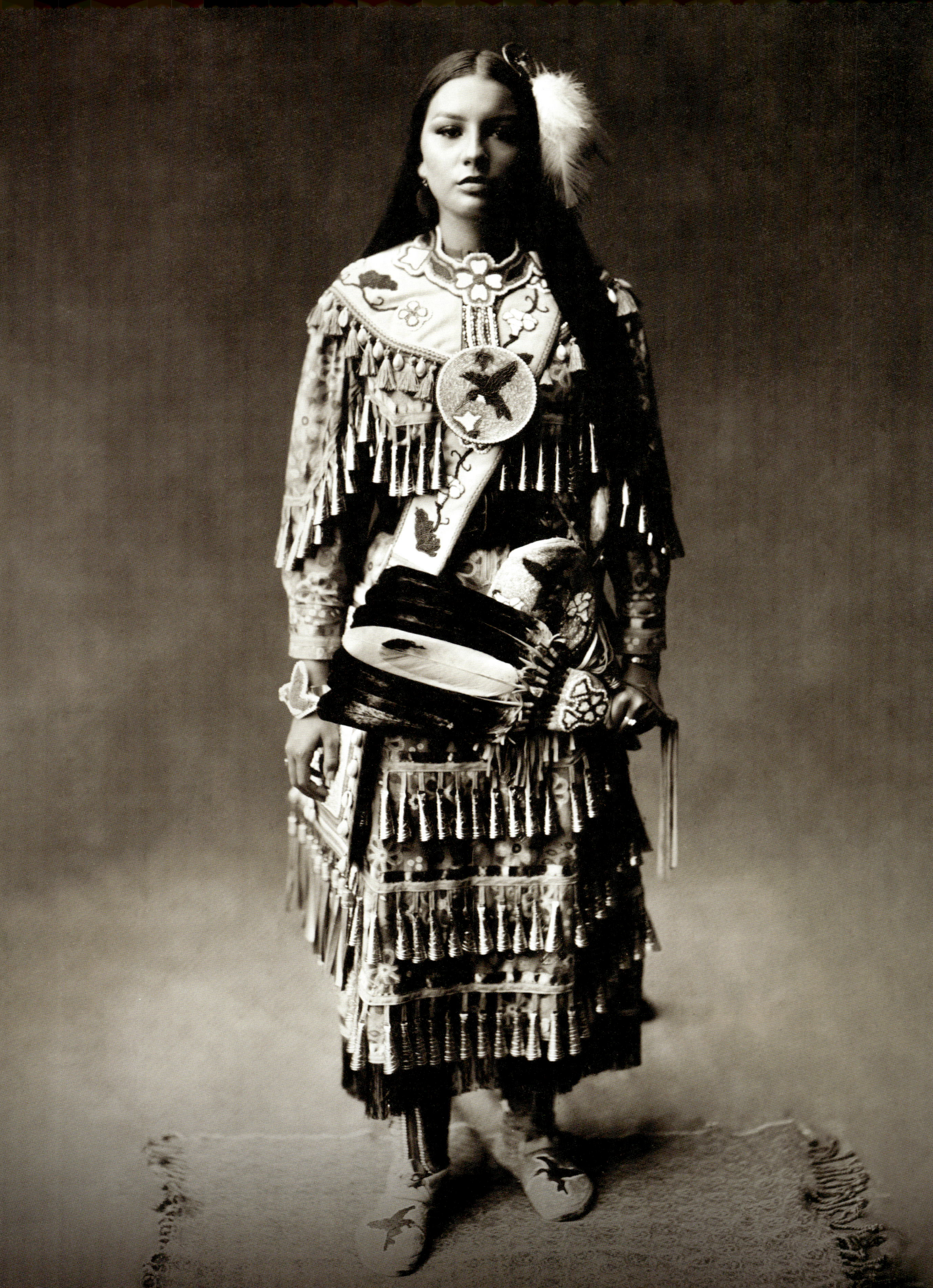

"Hummingbird" *Amari Opichi LaRocque* | Turtle Mountain Pembina Chippewa | 10 September 2021 | Plate No. 4018

"Red Road Woman" *Dakotah Rae Jourdain* | Crow Creek Sioux Dakota / Red Lake Ojibwe | 24 September 2021 | Plate No. 4038

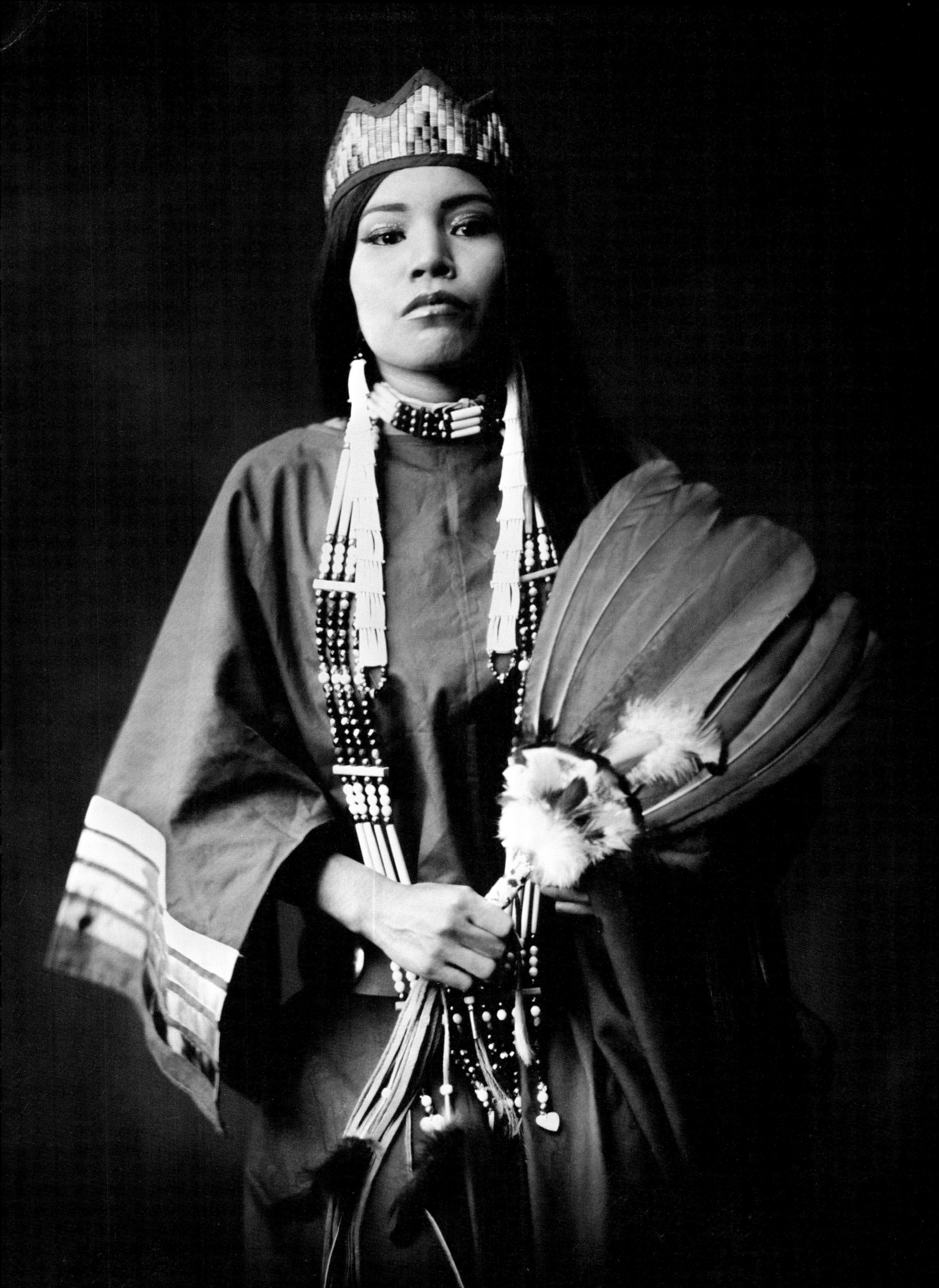

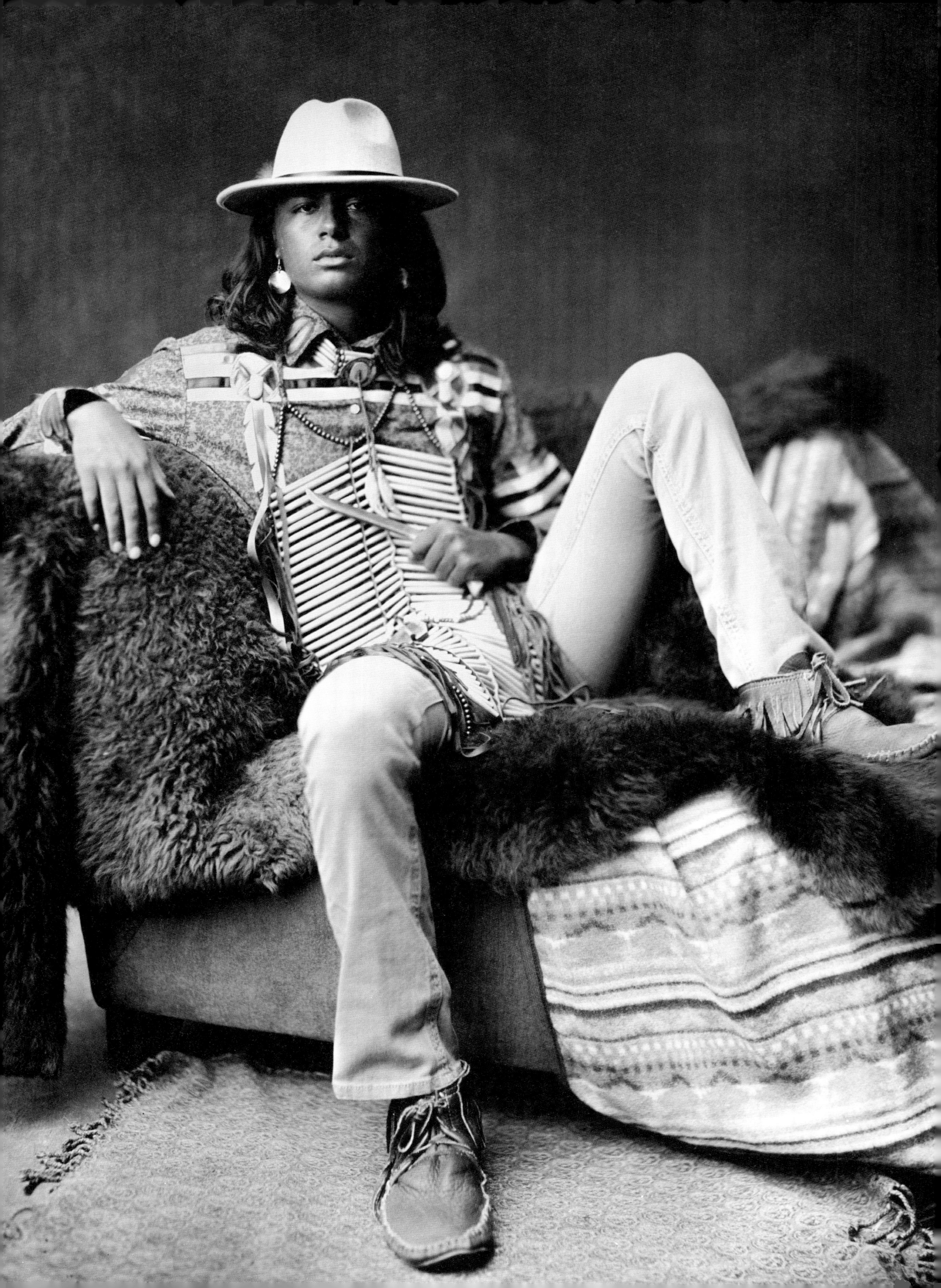

"Red Elk Whistling" *Clay Flying Eagle LaRocque* | Turtle Mountain Pembina Chippewa | 10 September 2021 | Plate No. 4022

"Thunder Wolf" *Jake Jordan Fox* | MHA Nation / Standing Rock Sioux | 9 June 2023 | Plate No. 4697

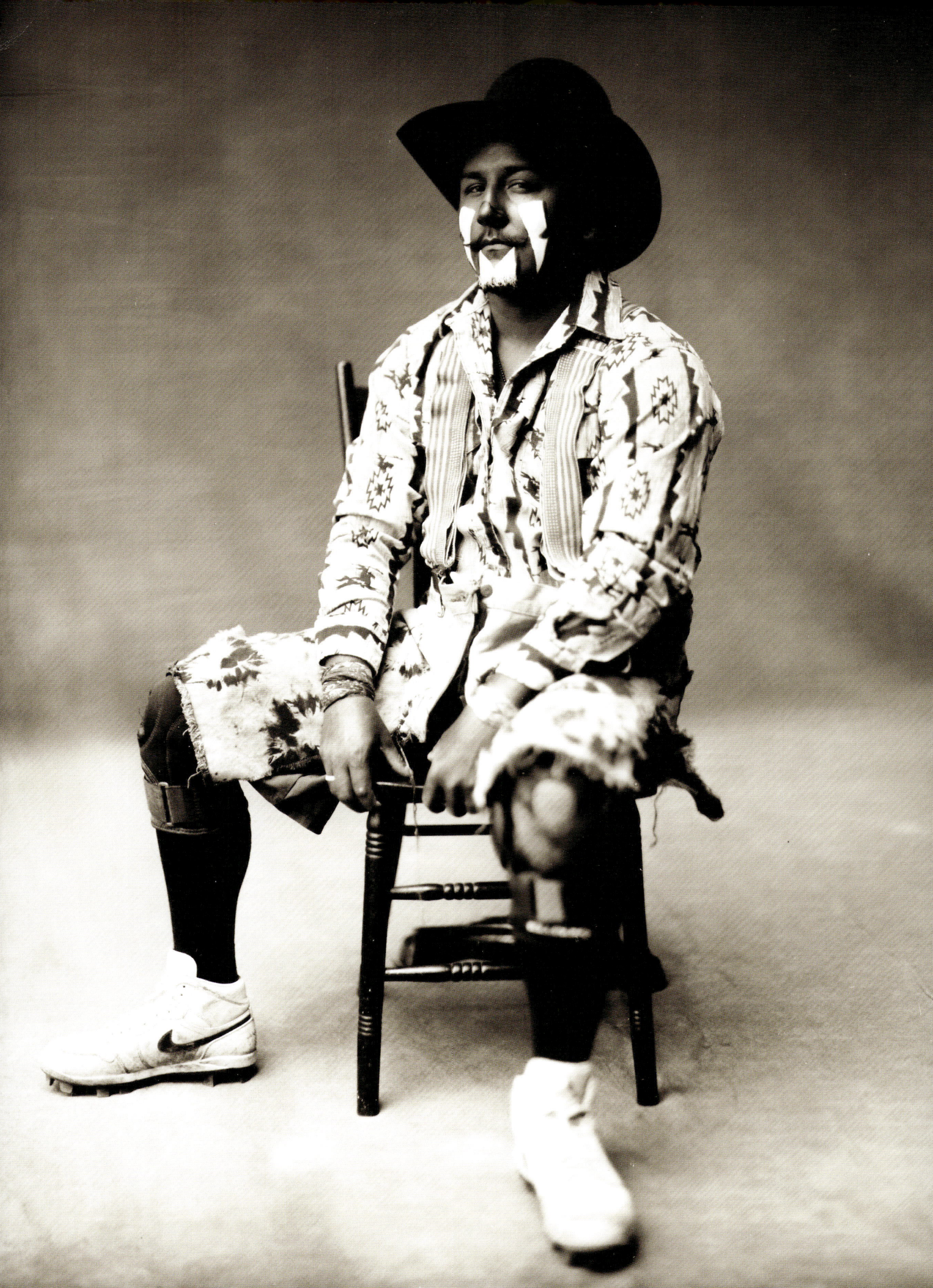

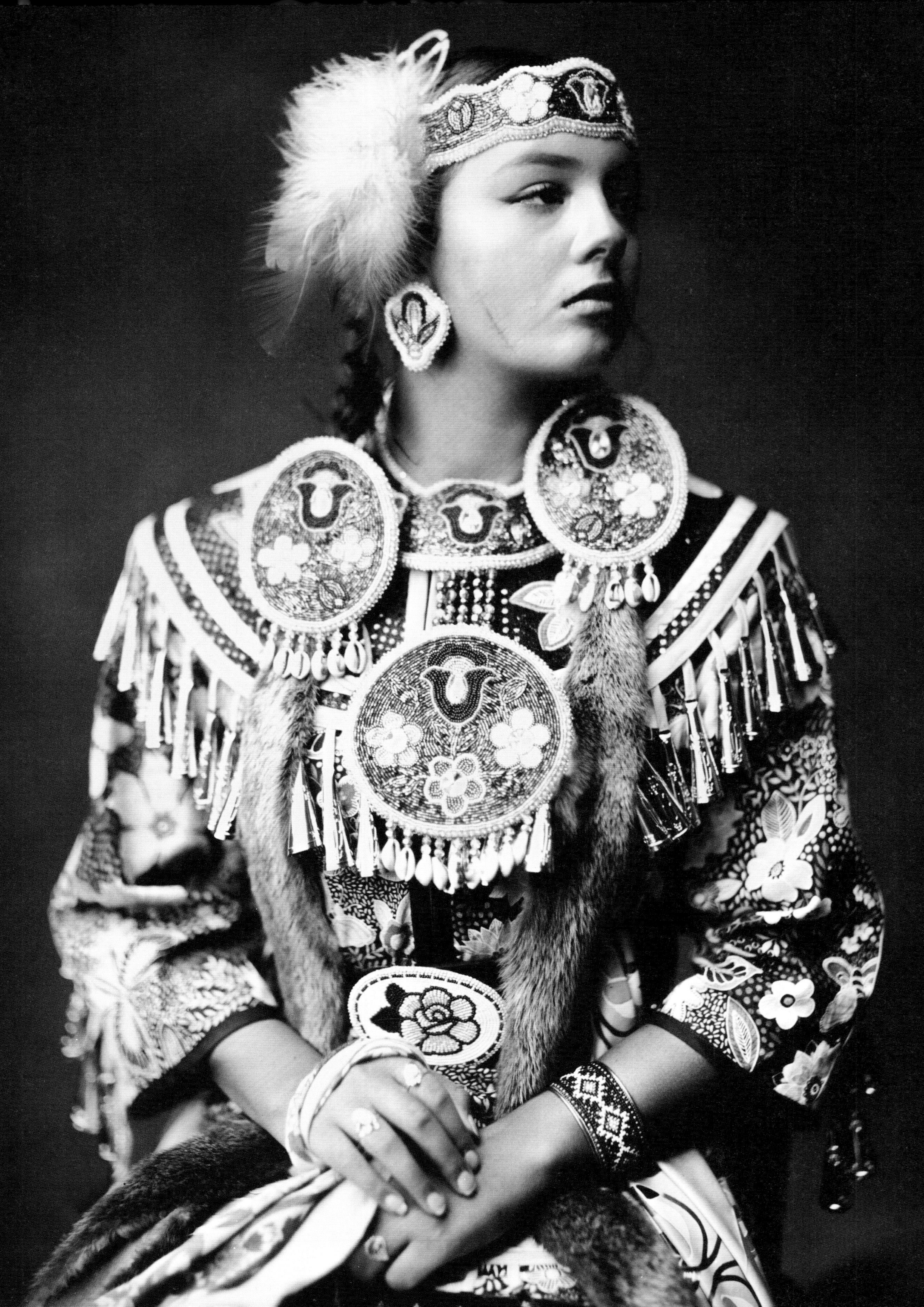

“Sheet Lighting” *Ashlin Quill LaRocque* | Turtle Mountain Pembina Chippewa | 10 September 2021 | Plate No. 4020

"Wild Horse" *Dennis Howling Wolf, Jr.* | Mandan / Hidatsa / Arikara | 20 January 2023 | Plate No. 4525

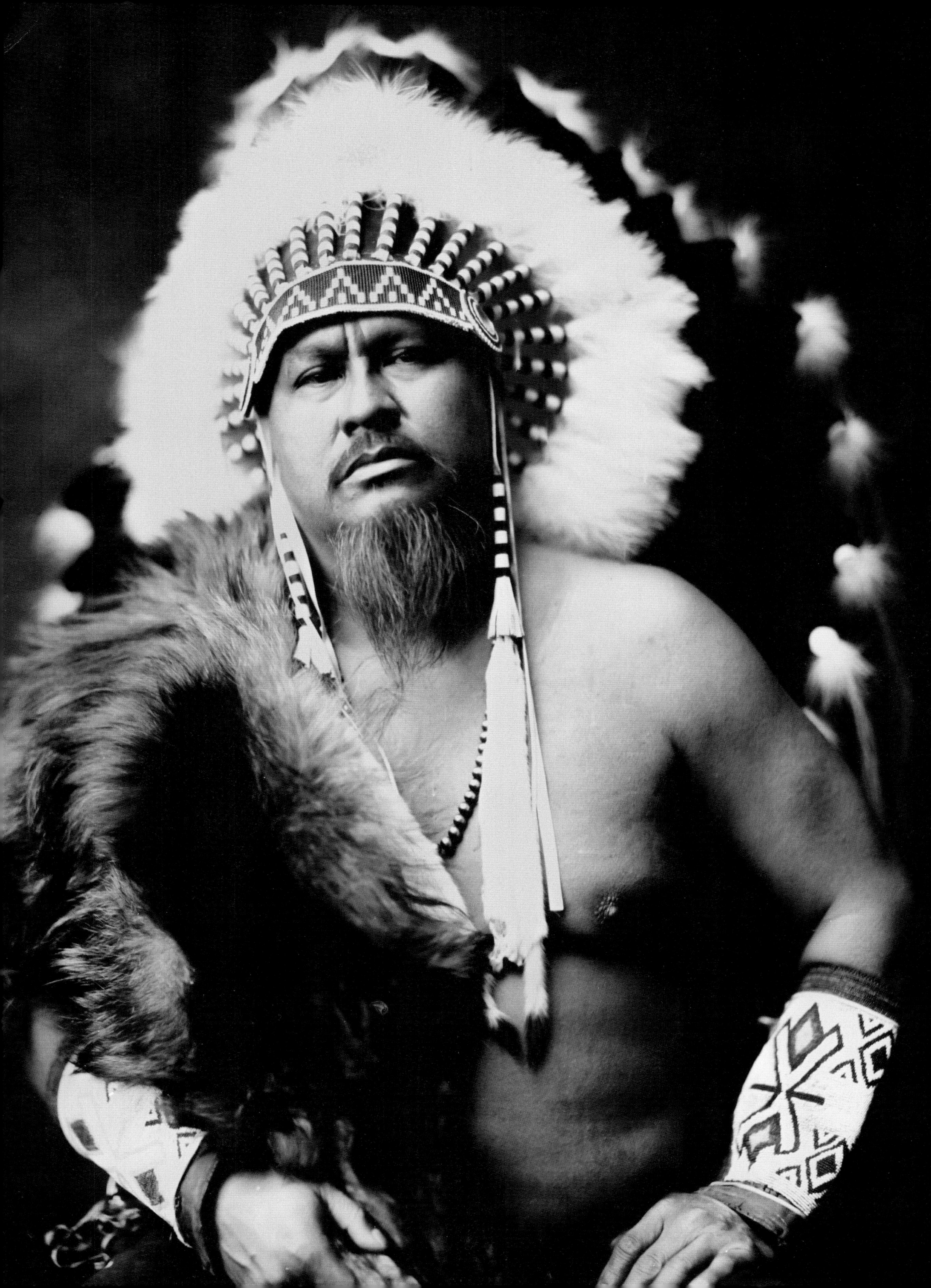

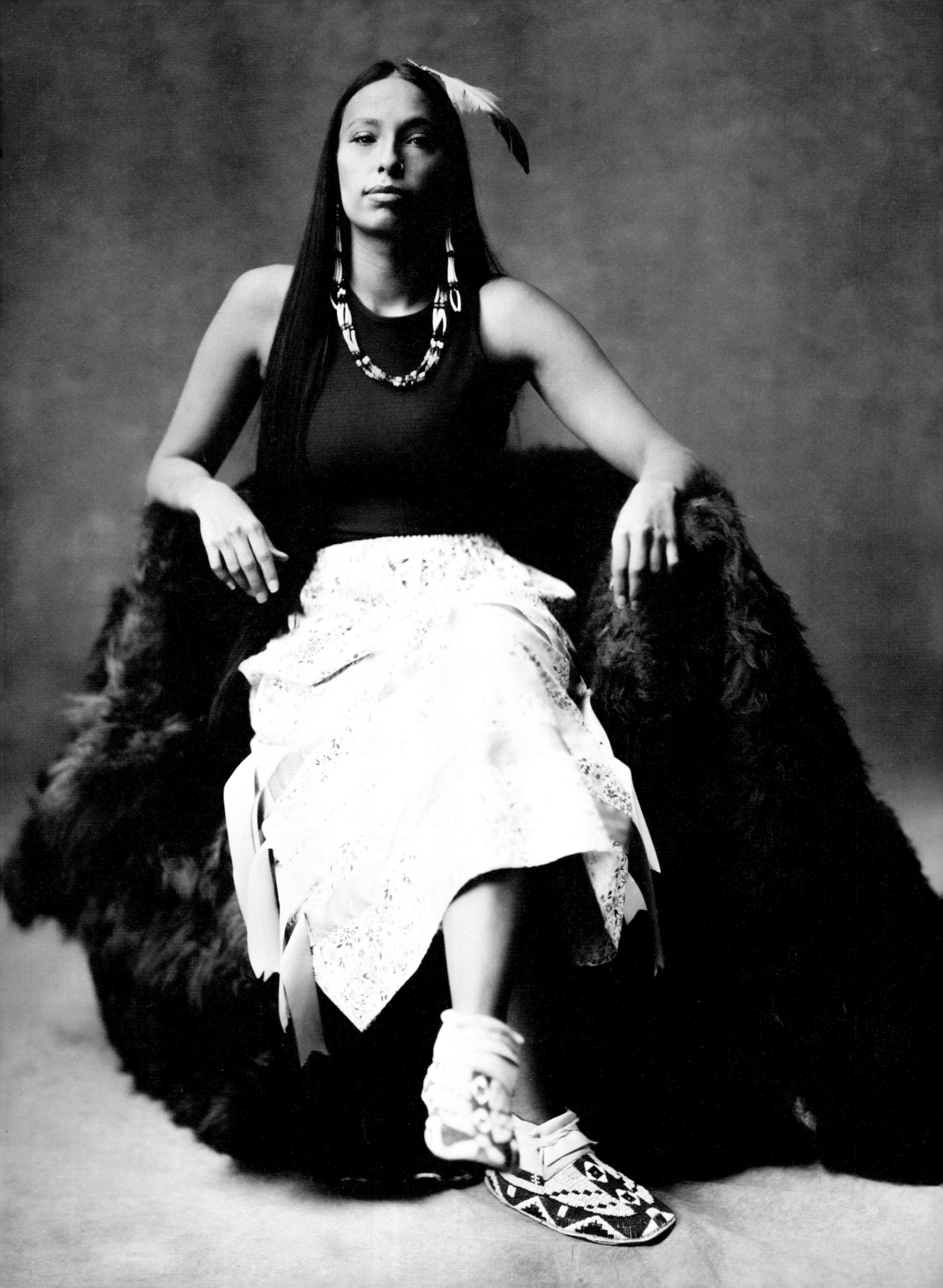

"Yellow Fox Woman" *Sidney Jo Bechtold* | Rosebud Sioux | 18 November 2022 | Plate No. 4472

“Smart” *Julianne Paige Smart* | Standing Rock Sioux | 7 October 2022 | Plate No. 4415

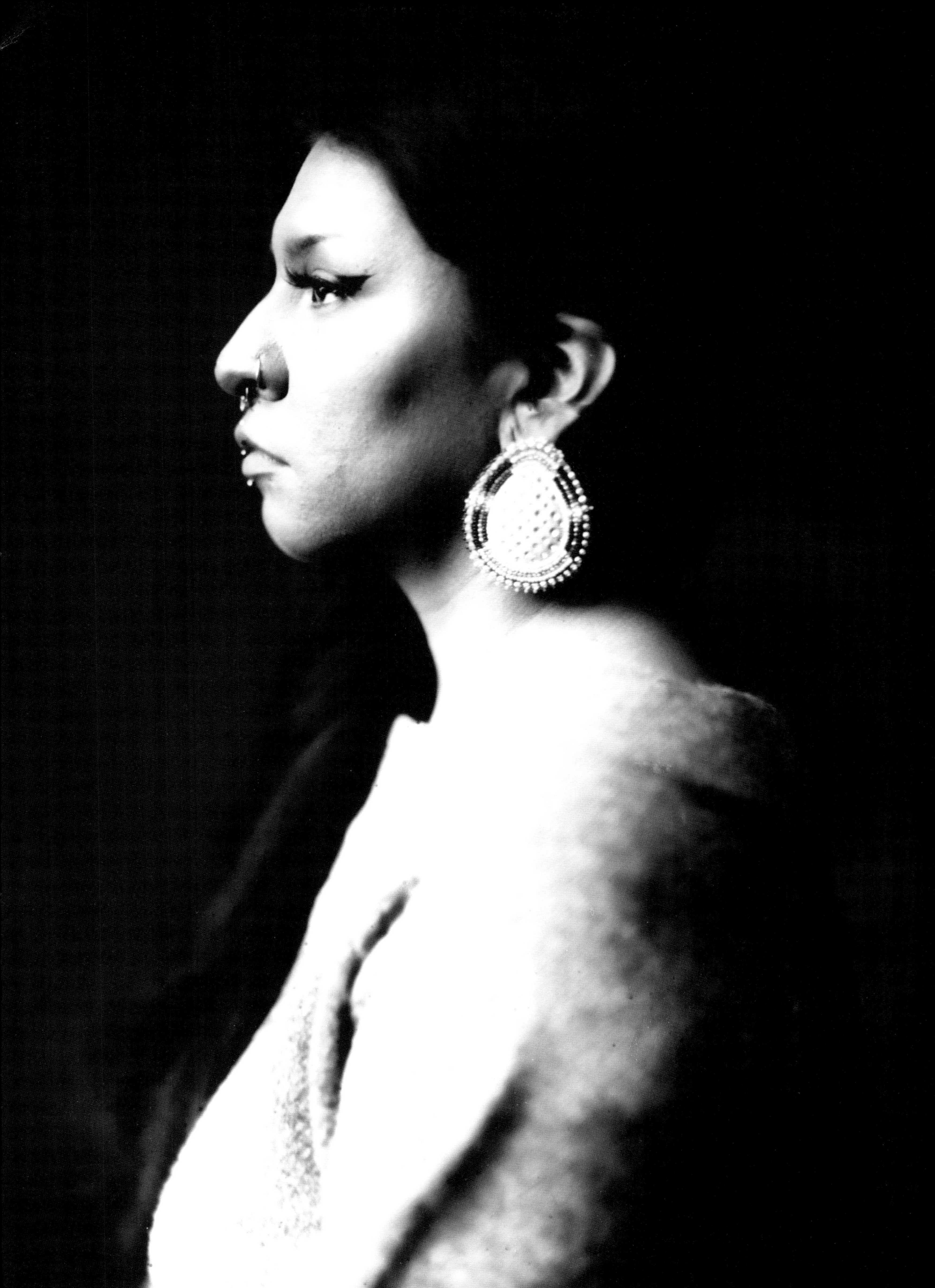

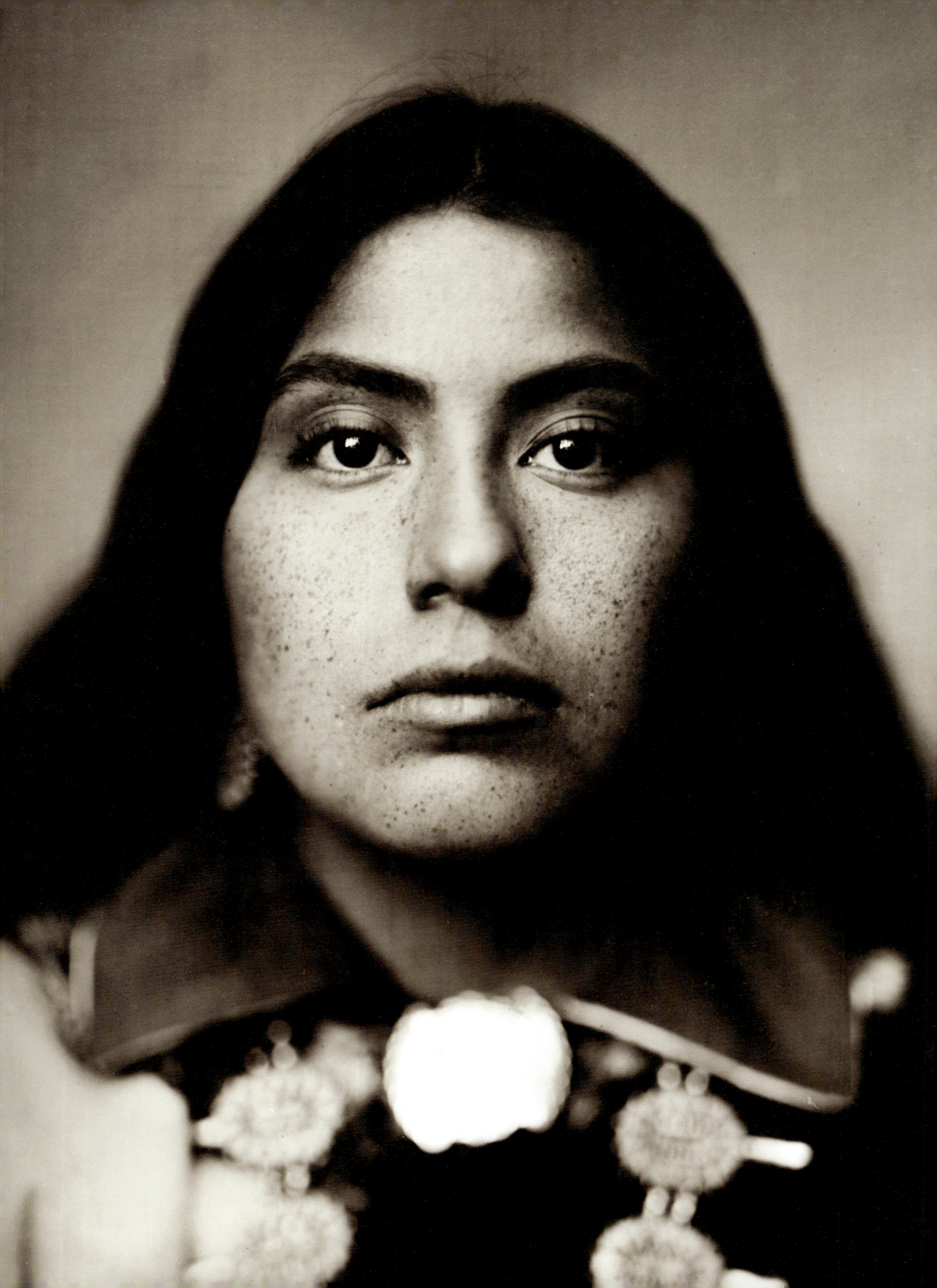

“Evergreen” *Lilly Chene Rose Dixon* | Hidatsa / Isleta Laguna Pueblo / Cochiti | 14 October 2022 | Plate No. 4431

“Cedar Roots Woman” *Loretta Mae DeLong, EdD* | Turtle Mountain Pembina Chippewa | 29 July 2022 | Plate No. 4340

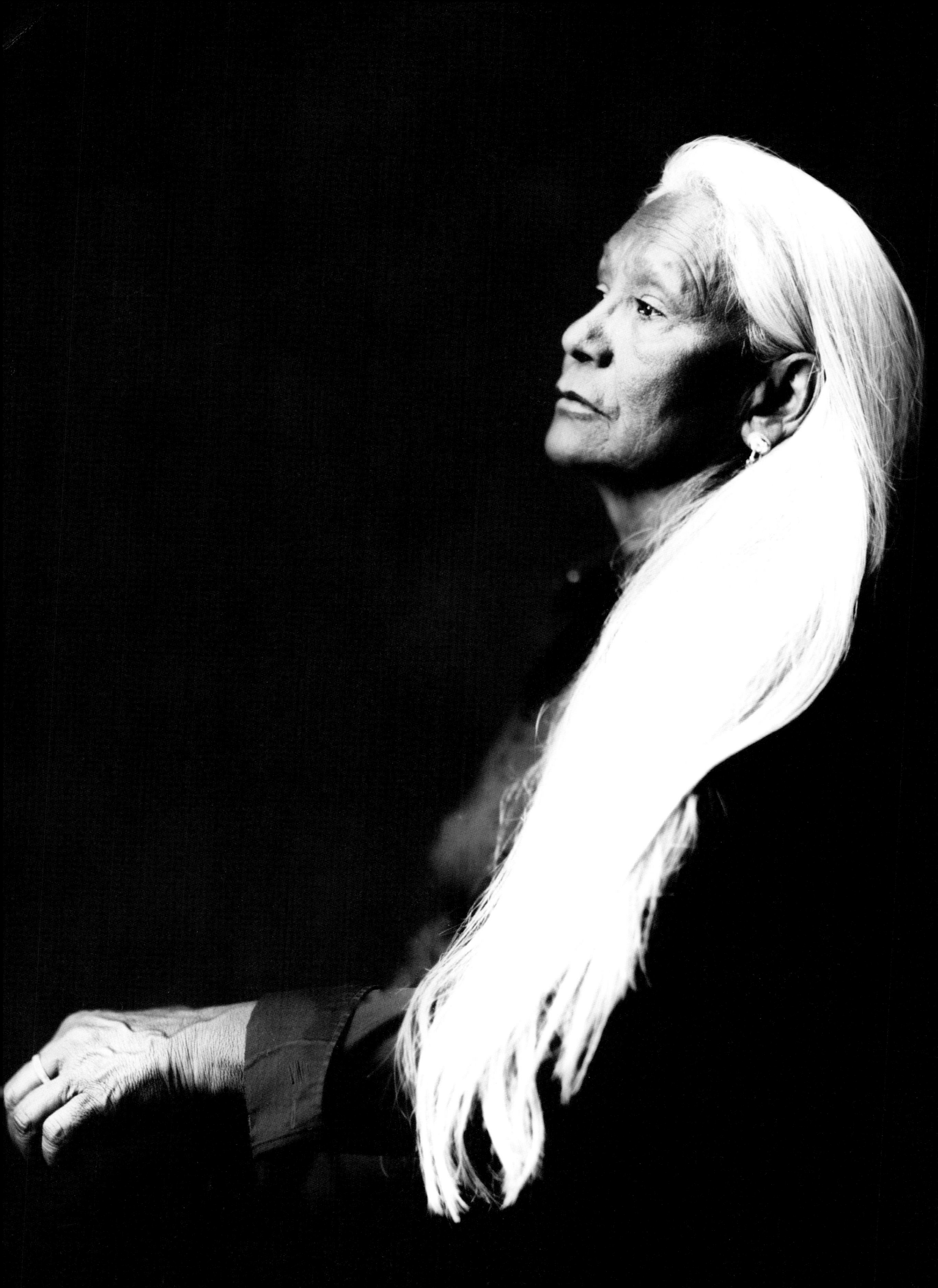

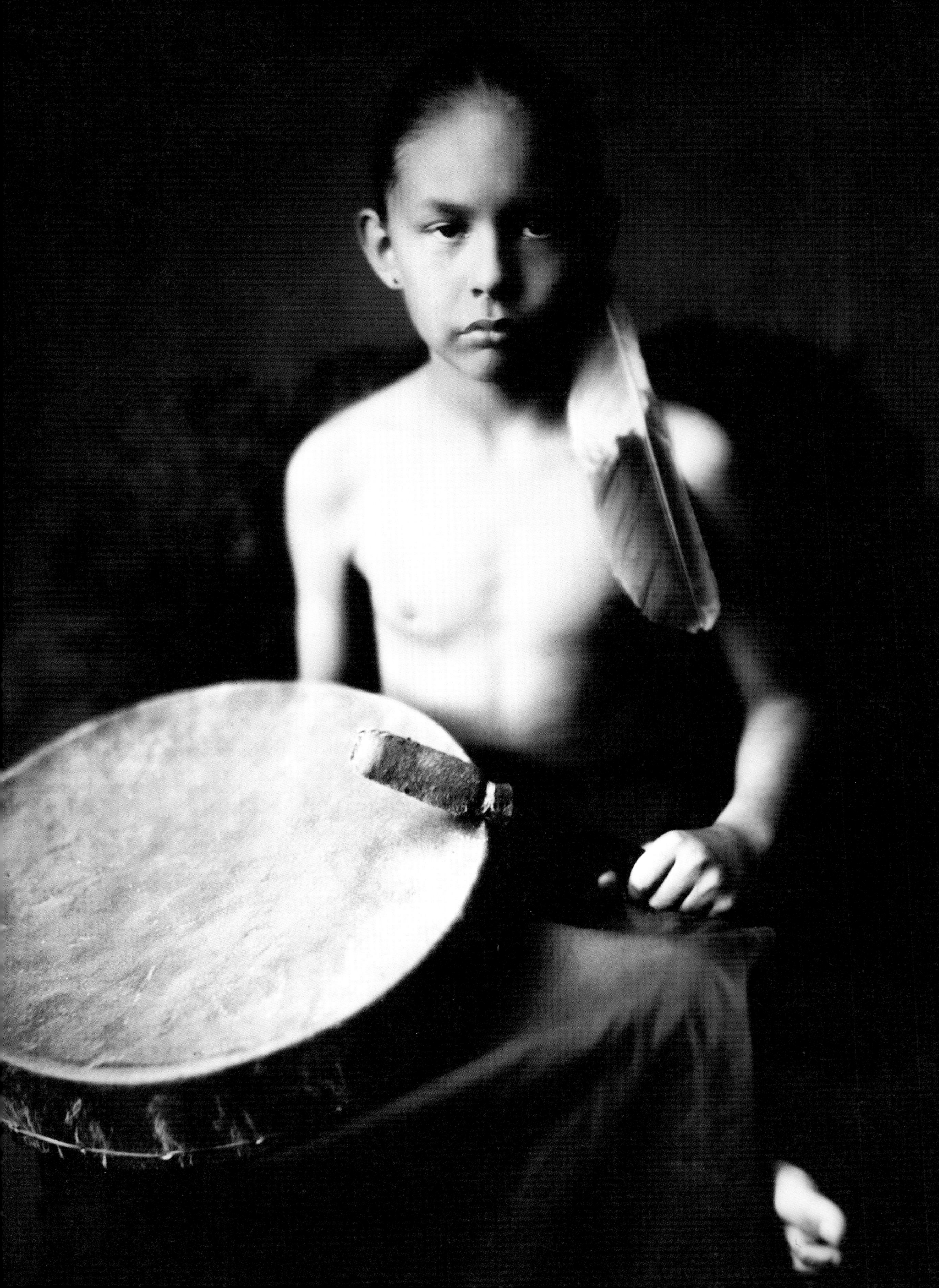

“Bear Heart” *Chante James Lambert* | Spirit Lake Dakota Nation | 4 November 2022 | Plate No. 4450

"The Man Who Stands In The Holy Lodge" *J. Garret Renville* | Sisseton Wahpeton Sioux / Omaha / Seneca | 3 March 2023 | Plate No. 4576

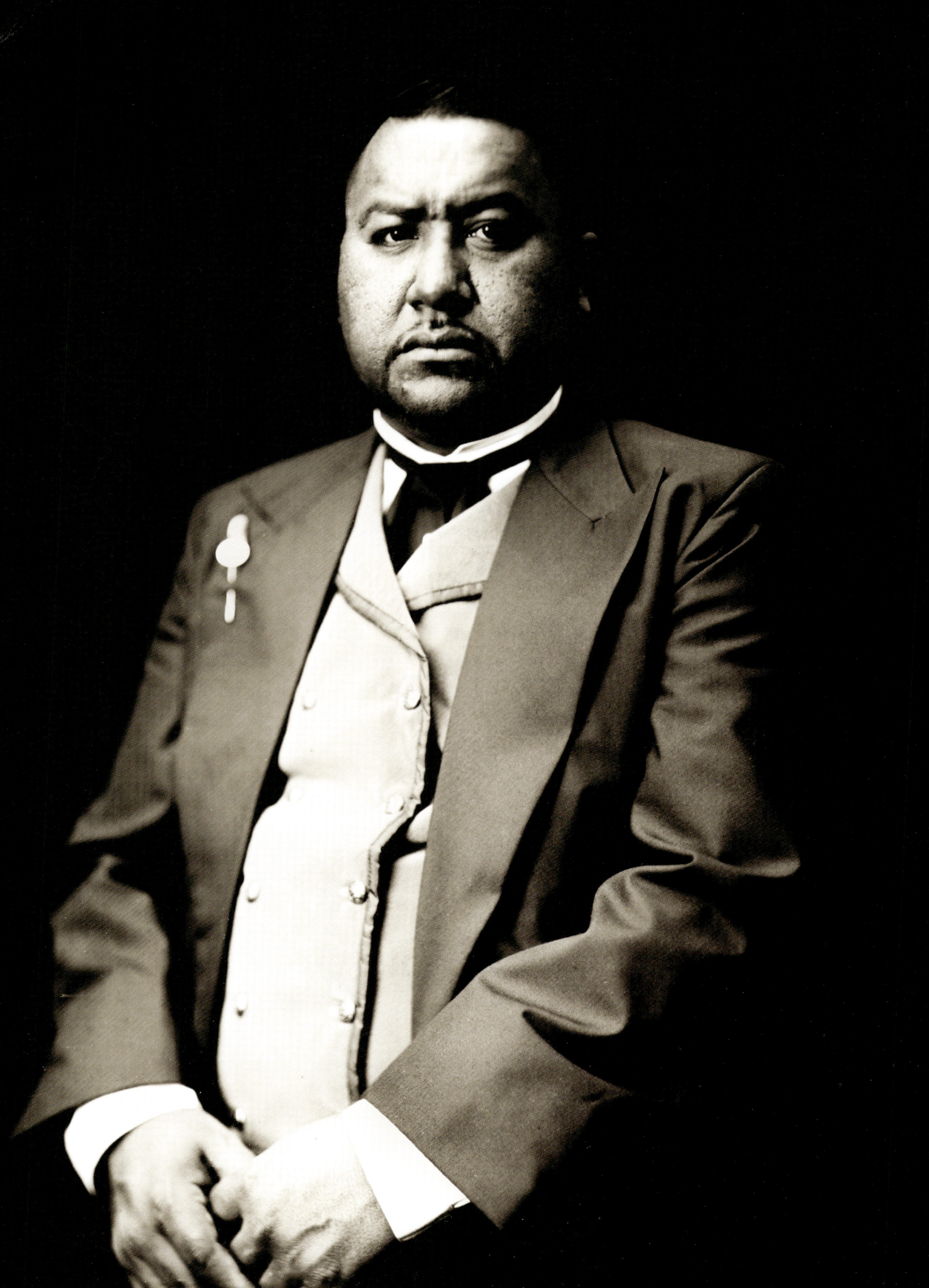

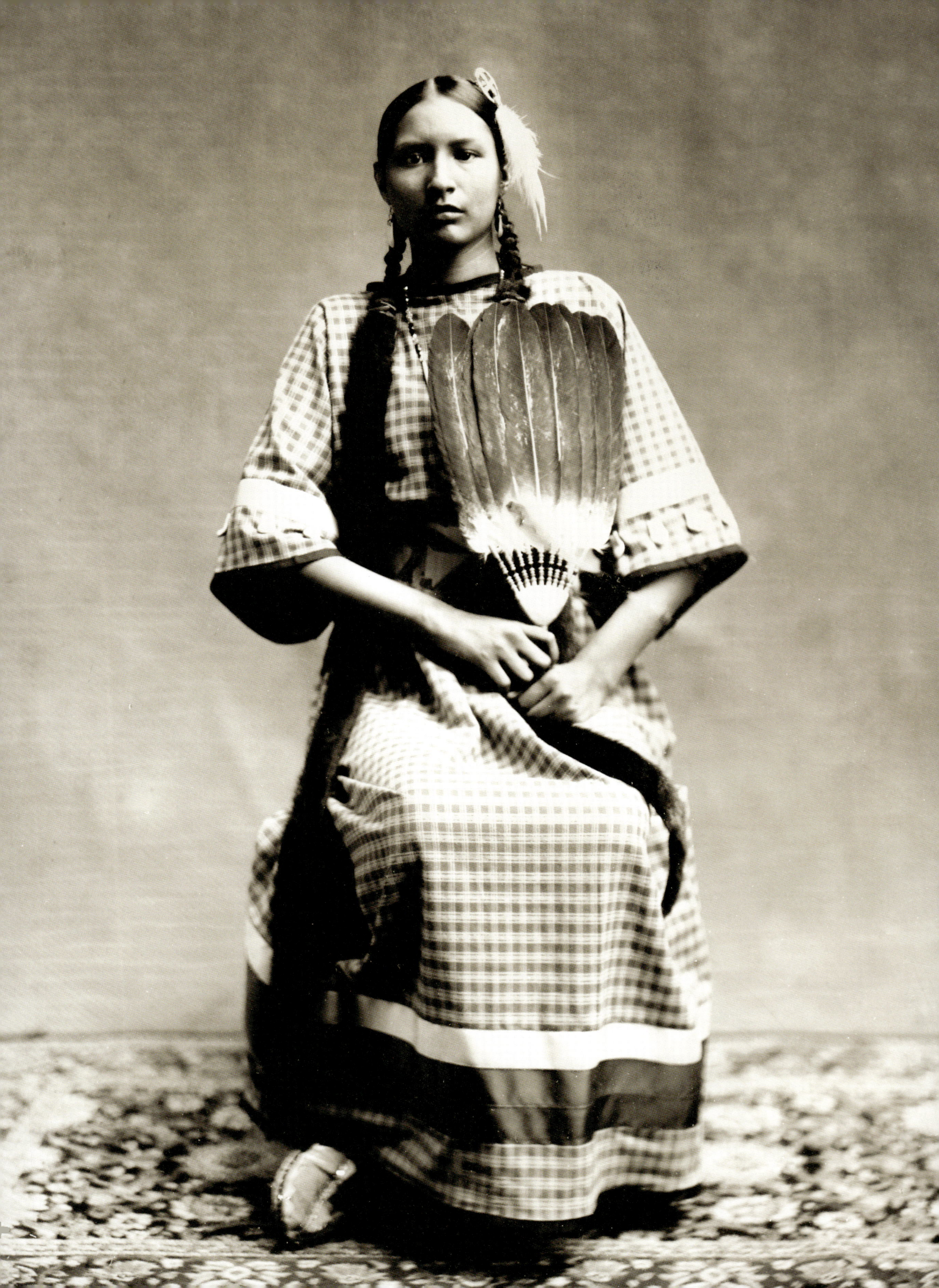

"Pretty Voice Crane Woman" *Lovelee Joy Holy Bull* | Spirit Lake Dakota / Cheyenne River Sioux | 14 April 2023 | Plate No. 4634

"White Headed Eagle" *Marcus Dominick Levings* | Mandan / Hidatsa / Arikara / Sioux, Yakama | 26 August 2022 | Plate No. 4364

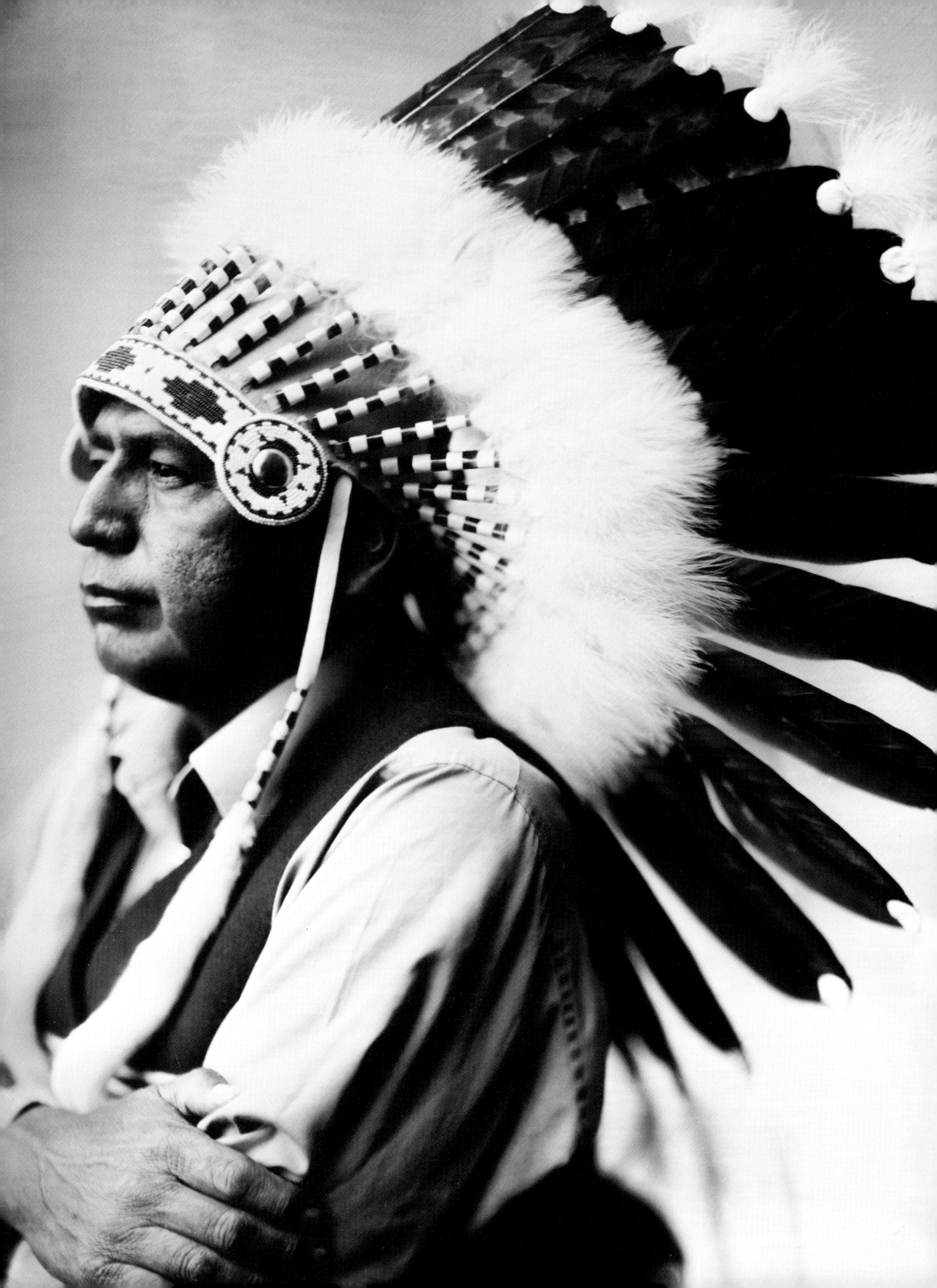

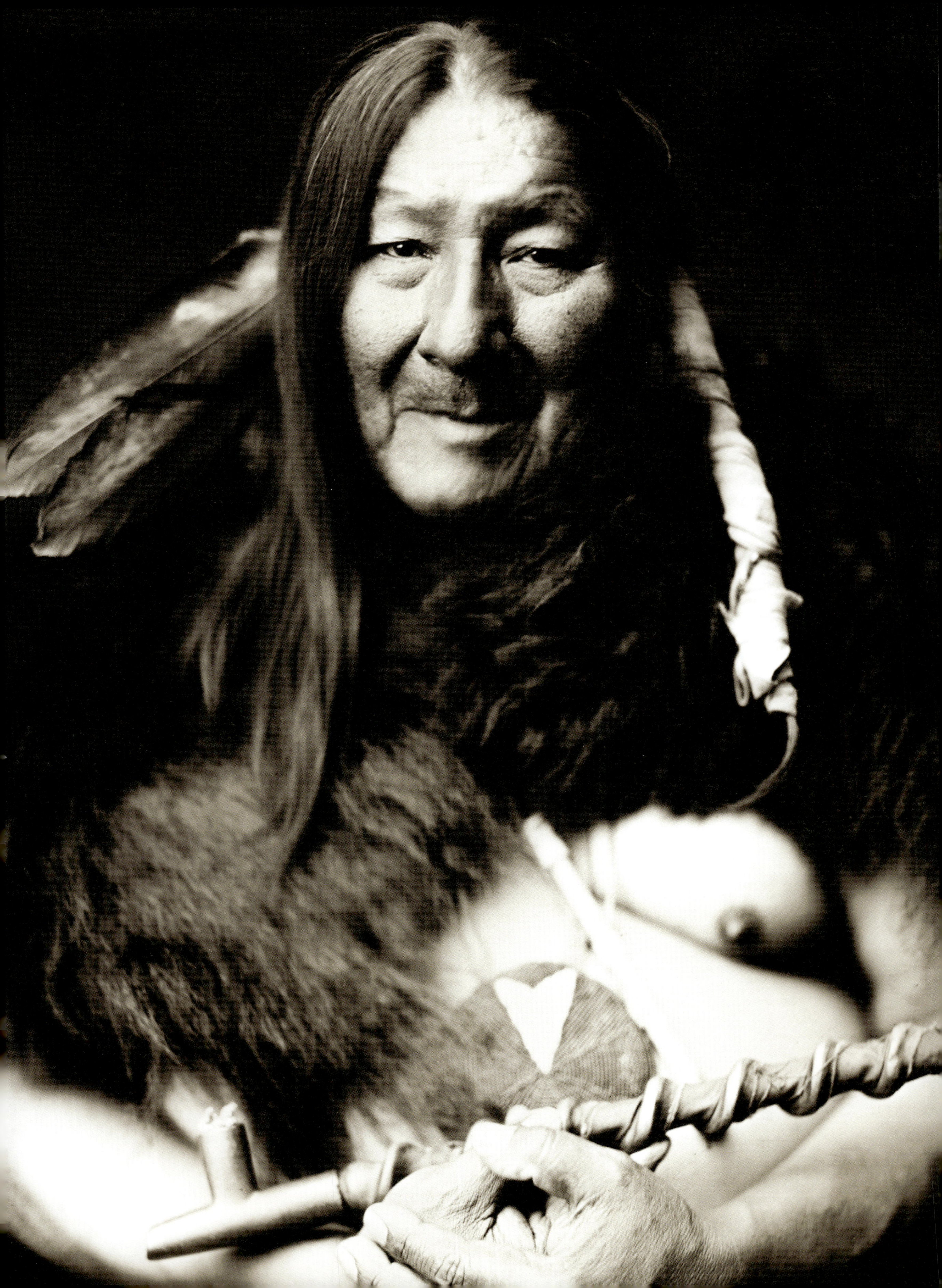

"Walks With Spotted Eagle Feather" *Michael Crandall Bissonette* | Oglala Sioux | 22 April 2022 | Plate No. 4230

"Loves By The Stars Woman" *Naomi Lillian Cross* | Hunkpapa / Oglala | 6 October 2023 | Plate No. 4827

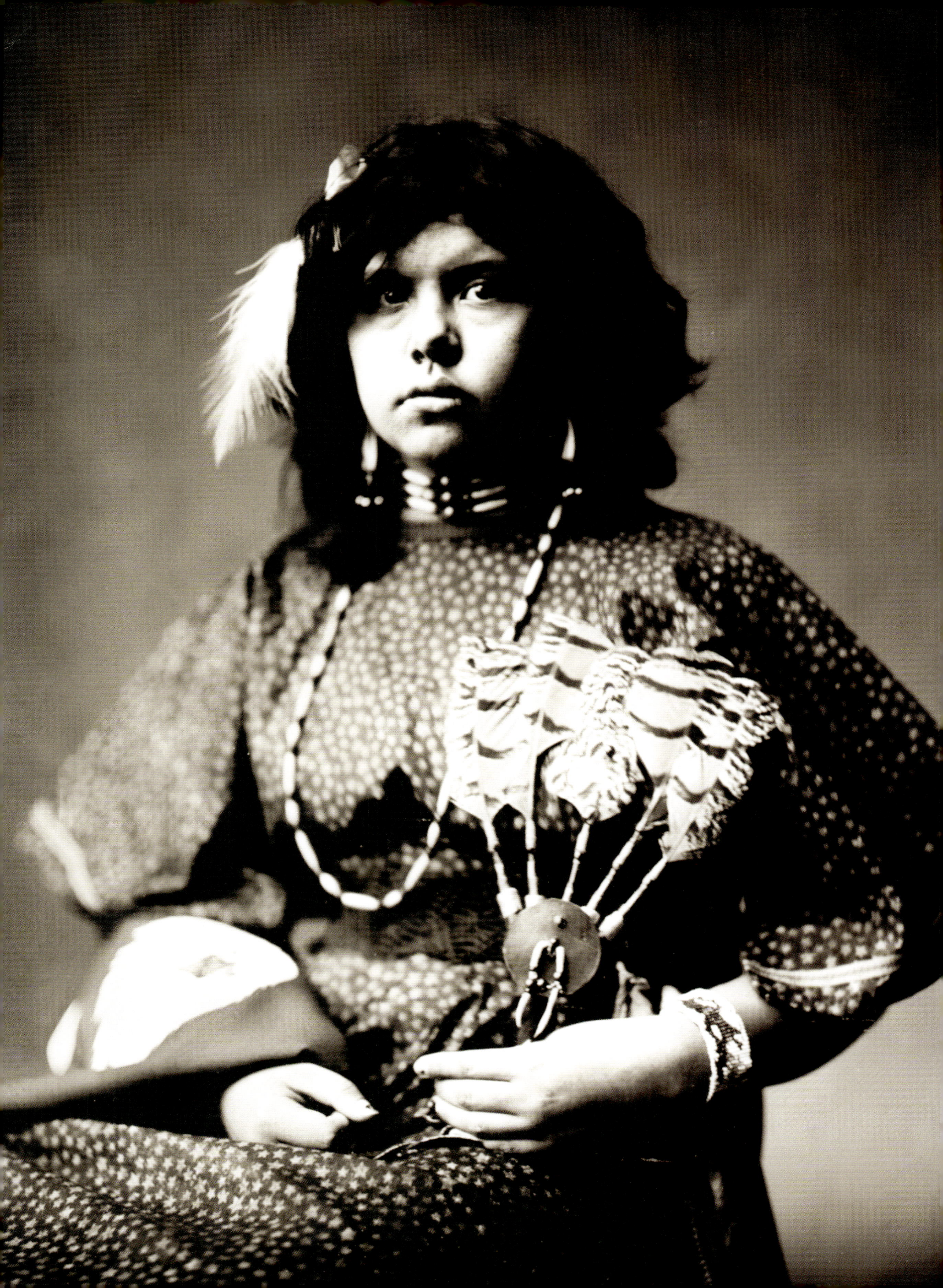

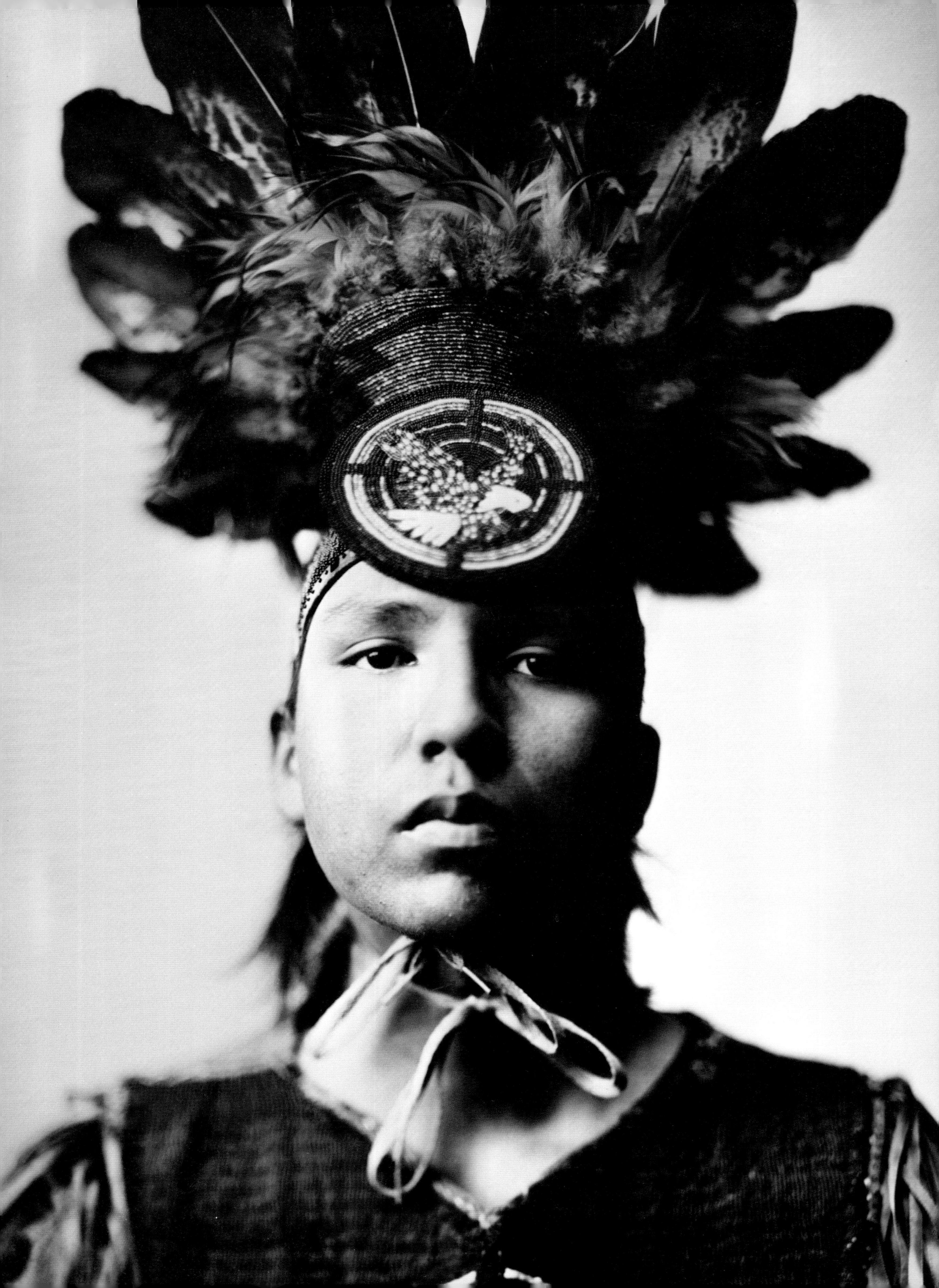

"Red Buffalo" *Caelen John Lohnes* | Spirit Lake Dakota Nation | 28 October 2022 | Plate No. 4443

“Big Bear” *Jeremy Lee Laducer* | Turtle Mountain Band of Chippewa | 28 April 2023 | Plate No. 4648

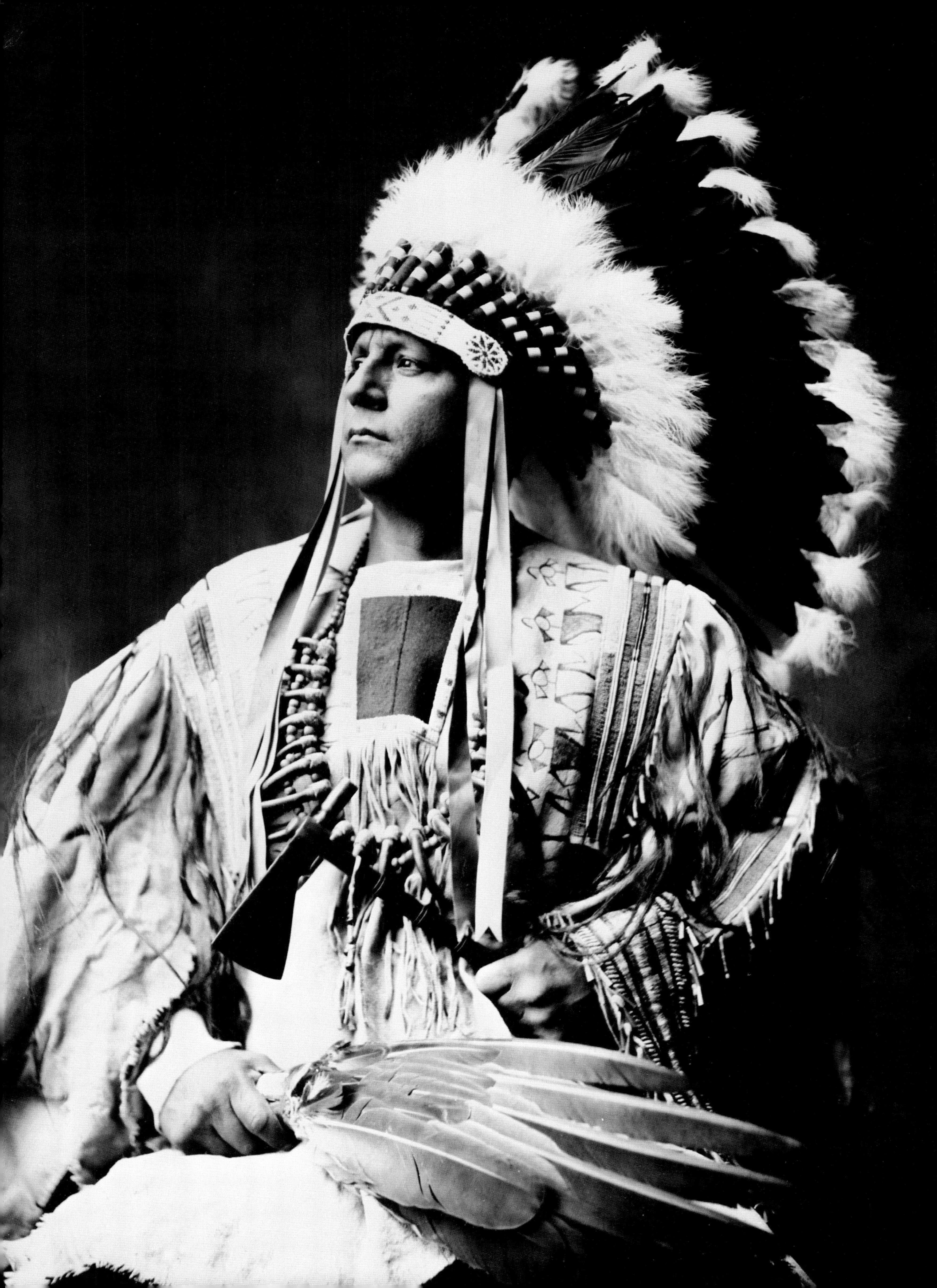

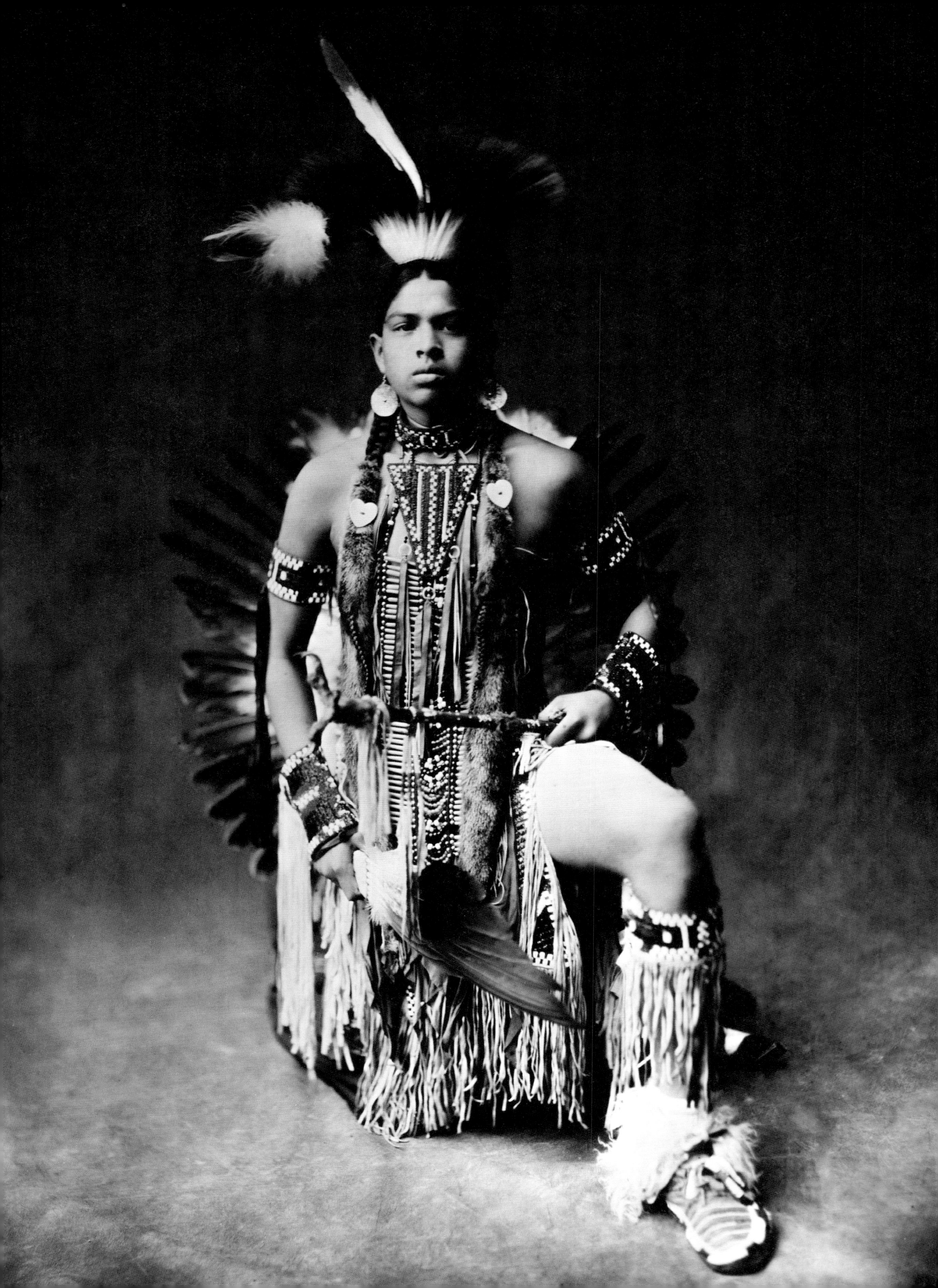

“Sacred Bear” *Redsky Starr* | Mandan / Hidatsa / Arikara / Yankton Sioux | 9 September 2022 | Plate No. 4387

"People Depends On Her" *Shawntay Rosemary Iron Horse* | Oglala Lakota | 10 September 2021 | Plate No. 4015

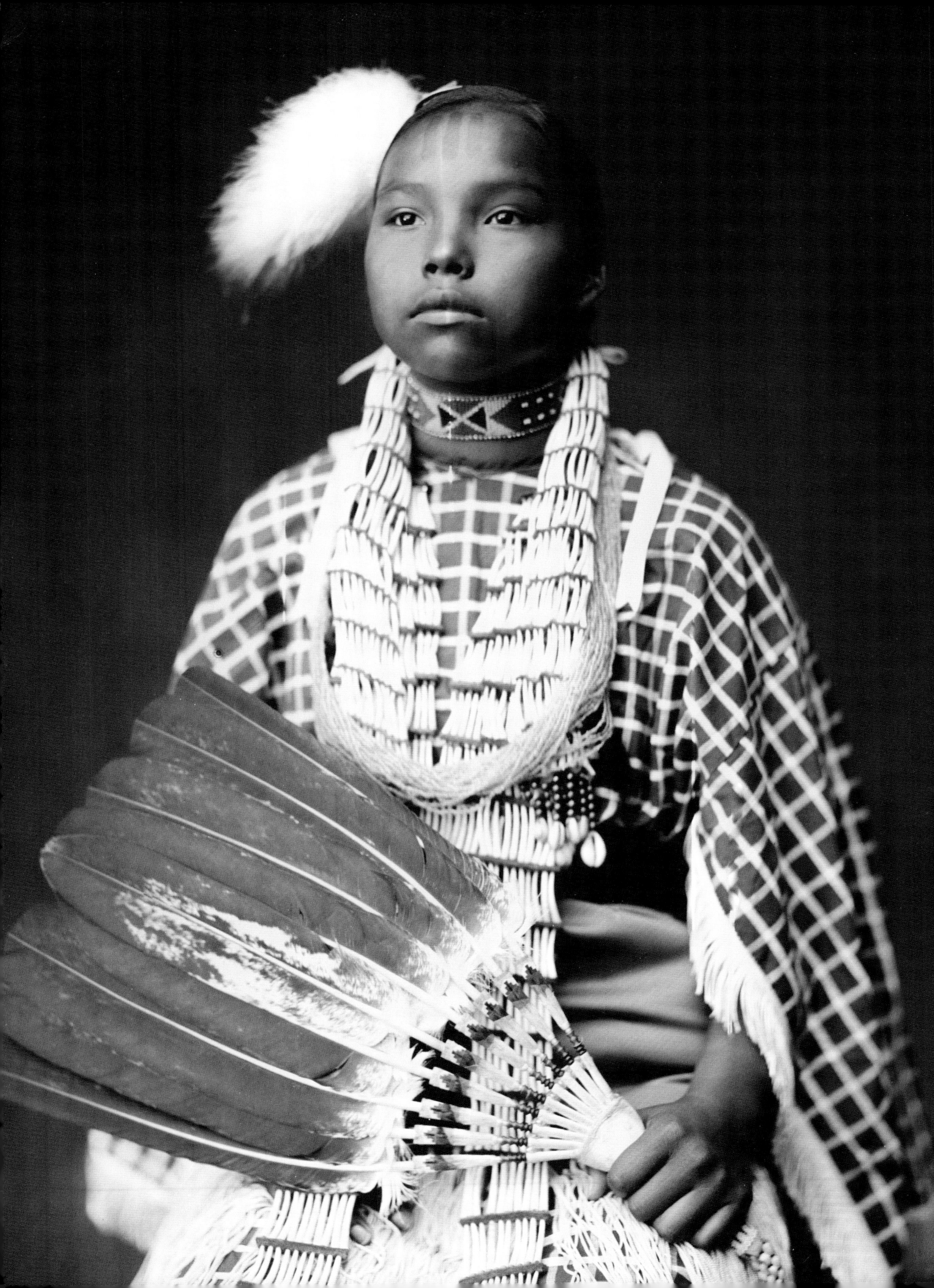

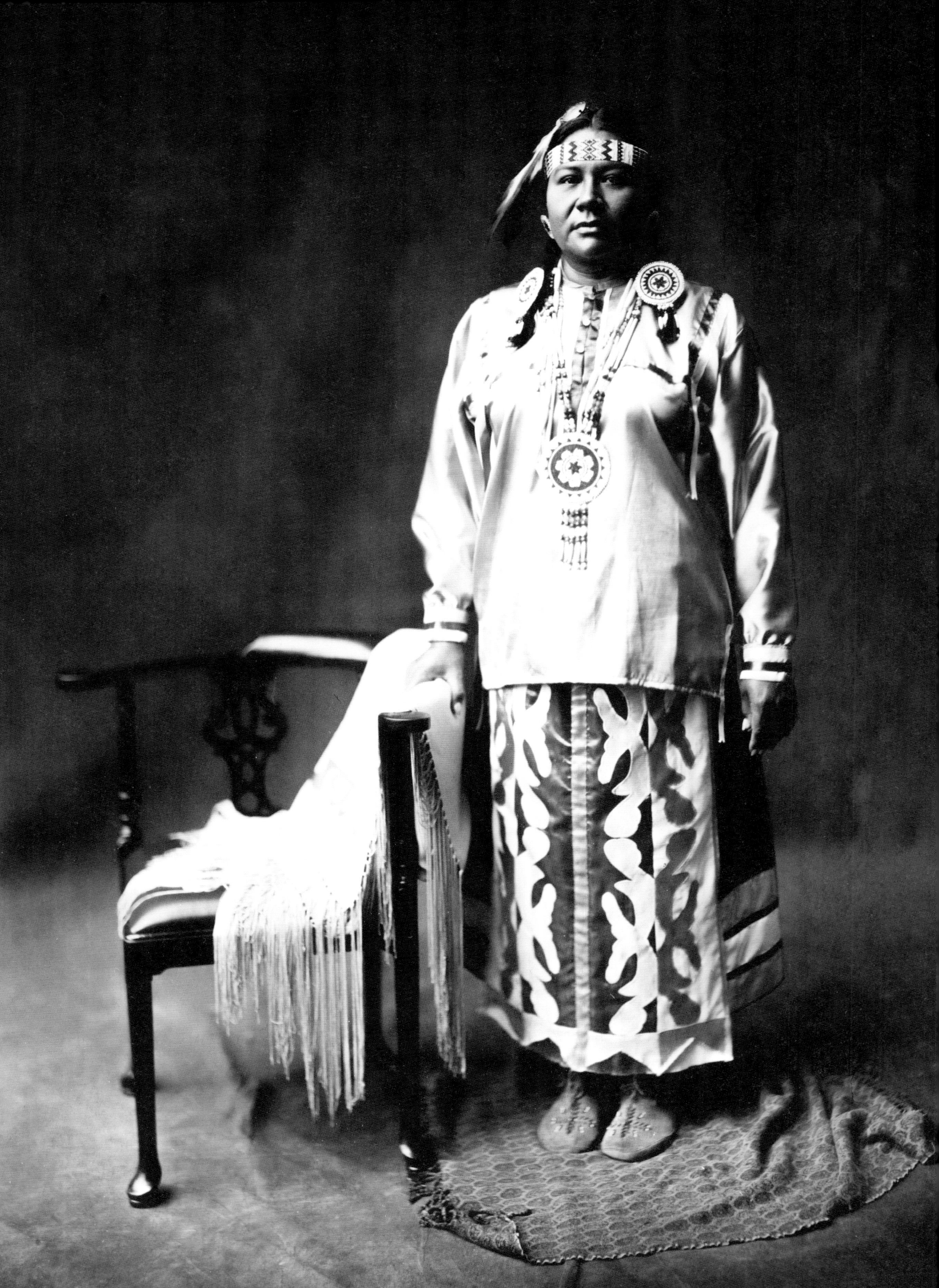

"Bayokia" *Misty Blue Young Bear, RN* | Meskwaki / Omaha | 19 August 2022 | Plate No. 4357

"White Ermine" *Siliye Tiznahbah Pete* | Bitter Root Salish / Navajo / Klamath | 4 February 2022 | Plate No. 4146

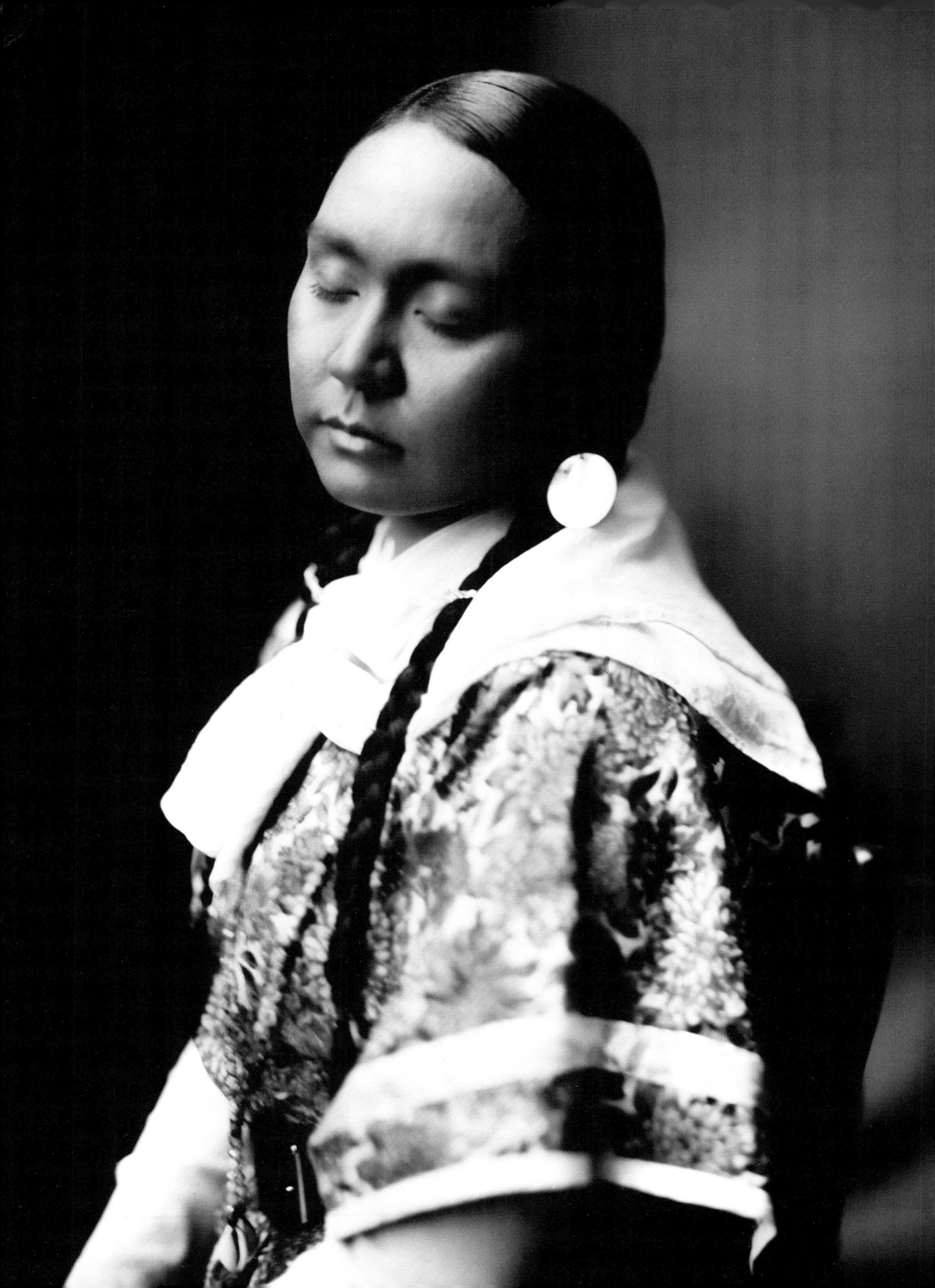

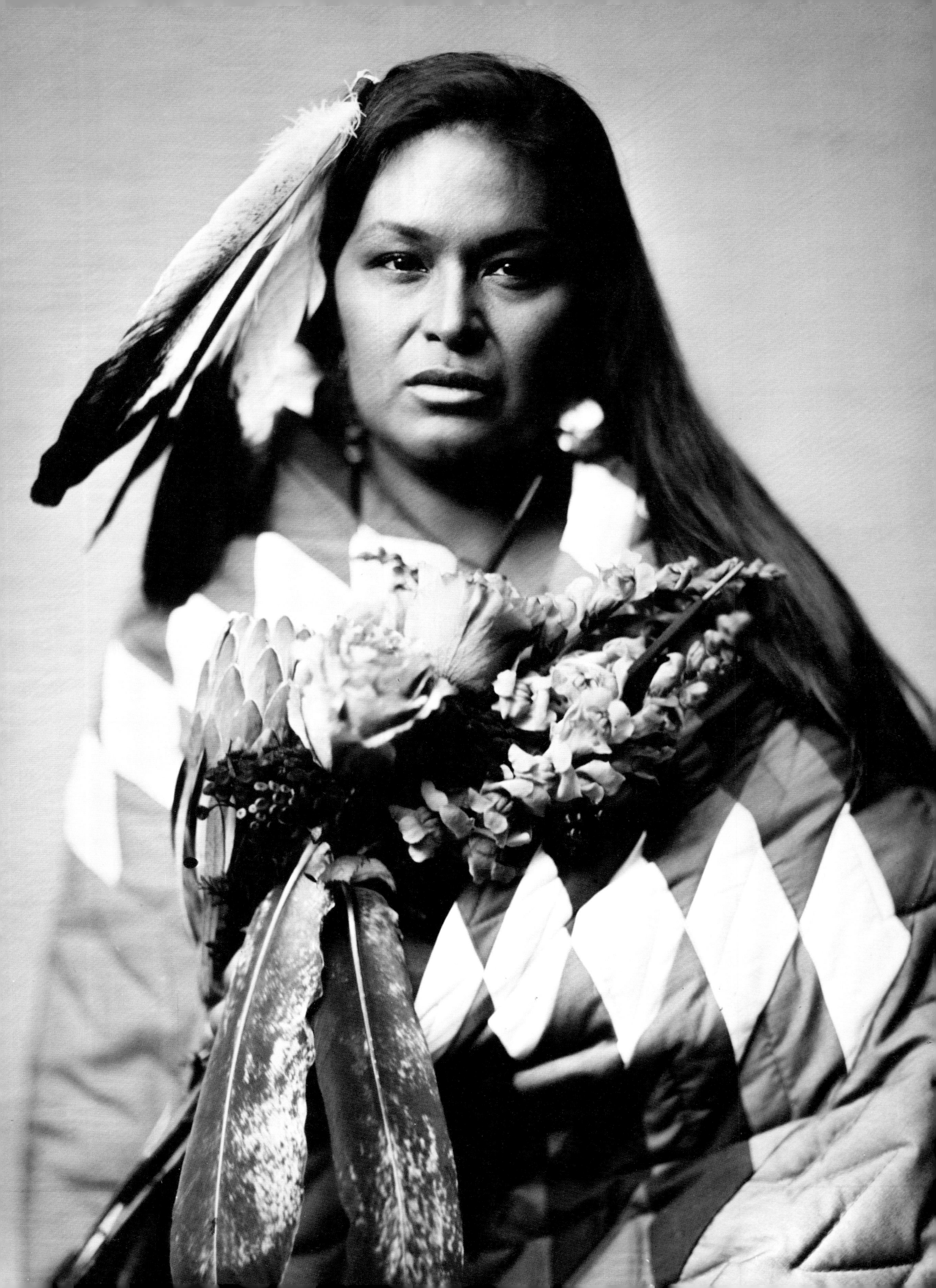

"Happiness Bringer Of Joy" *Rika Daisy Lee Powaukee* | Nez Perce | 20 August 2021 | Plate No. 3991

“Snow Bird” *Snowbird Rodriguez* | Yaqui Yoeme / Apache | 3 September 2021 | Plate No. 4005

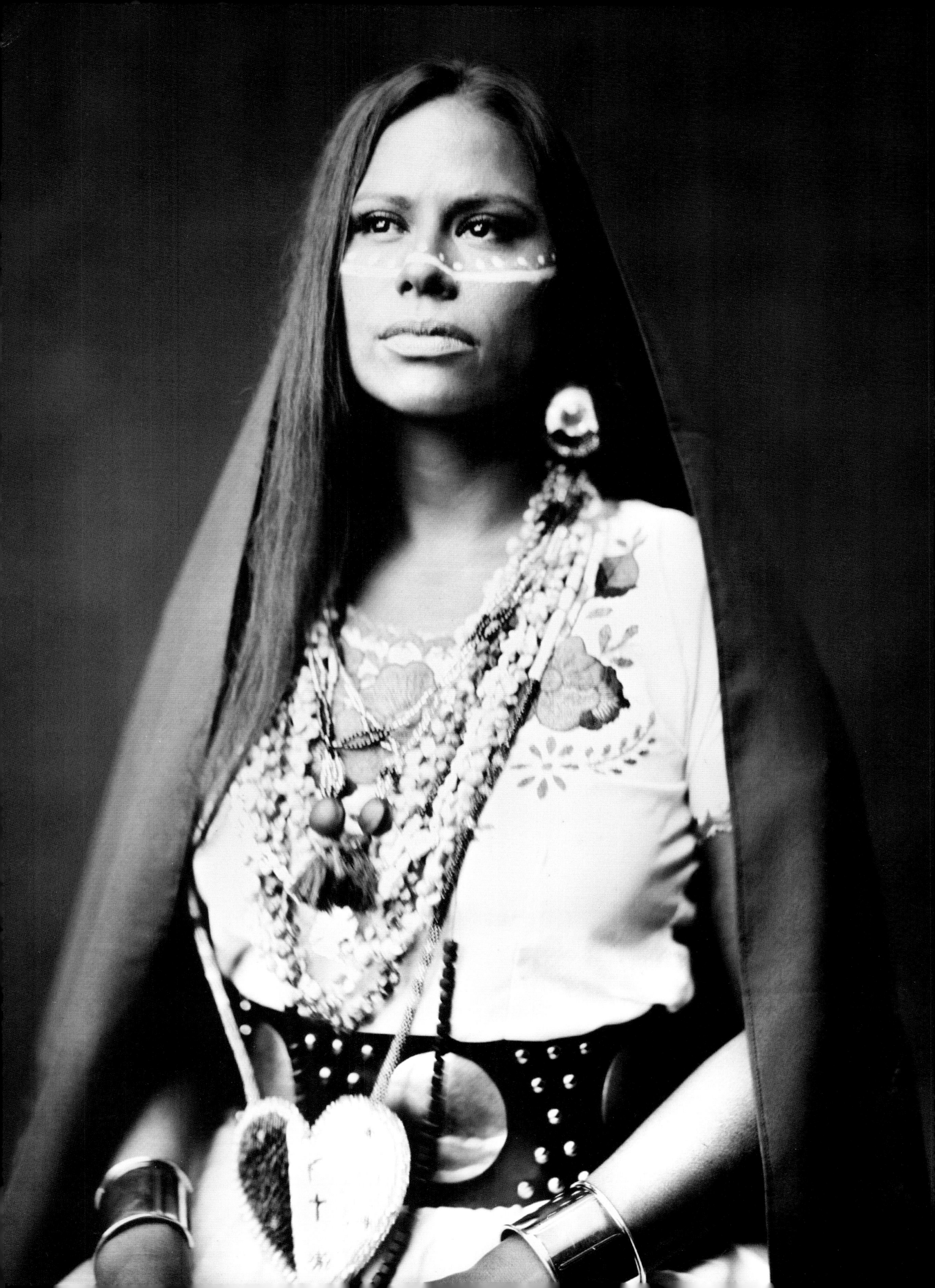

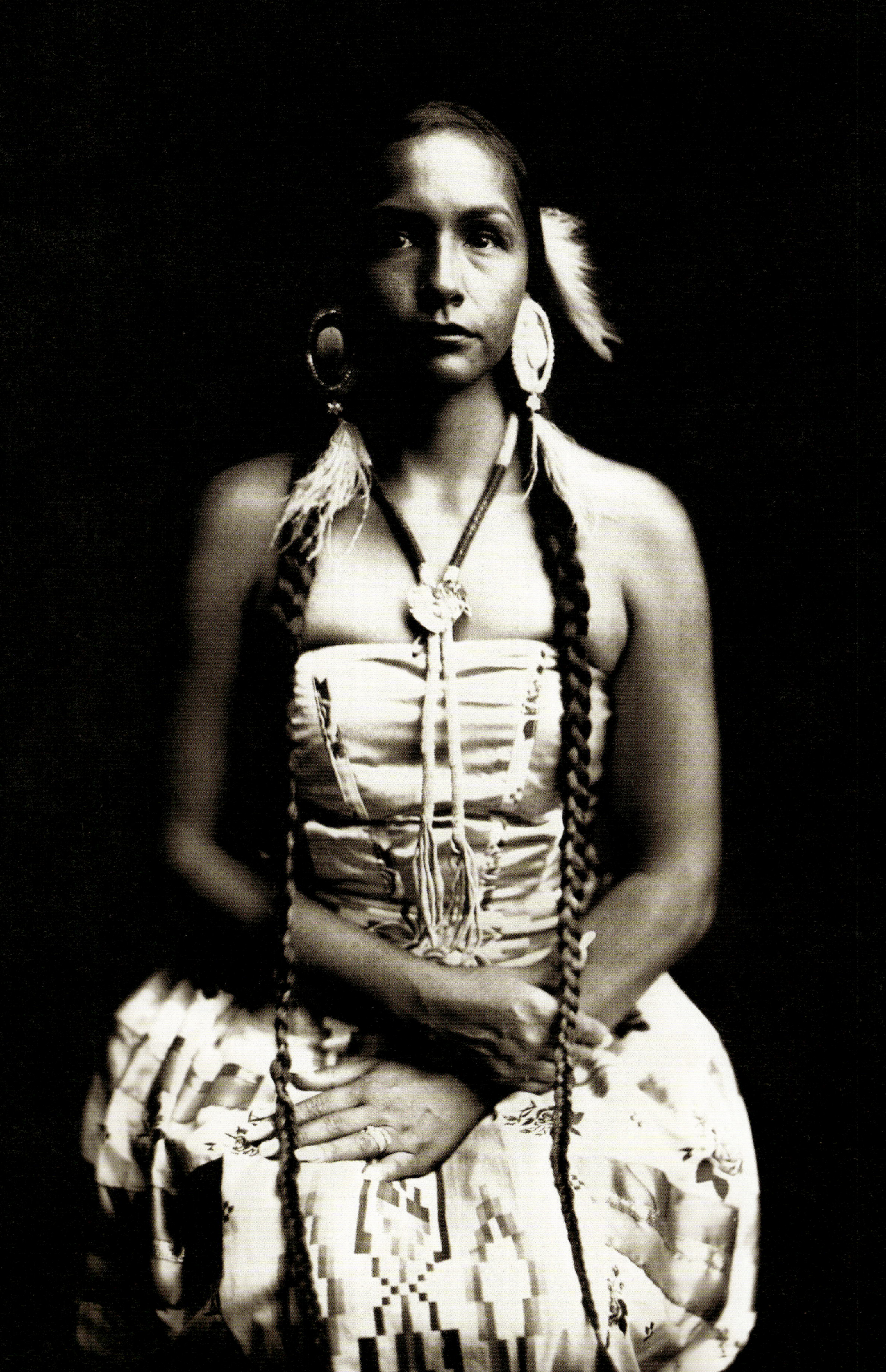

“Fighter Survivor Woman” *Seneca Jade Skunk* | Lower Brule Sioux / Lakota | 4 August 2023 | Plate No. 4750

“Early Light Woman” *Sylvia Julia Joanna Bissonette.* | Oglala / Grand Traverse Chippewa | 21 October 2022 | Plate No. 4435

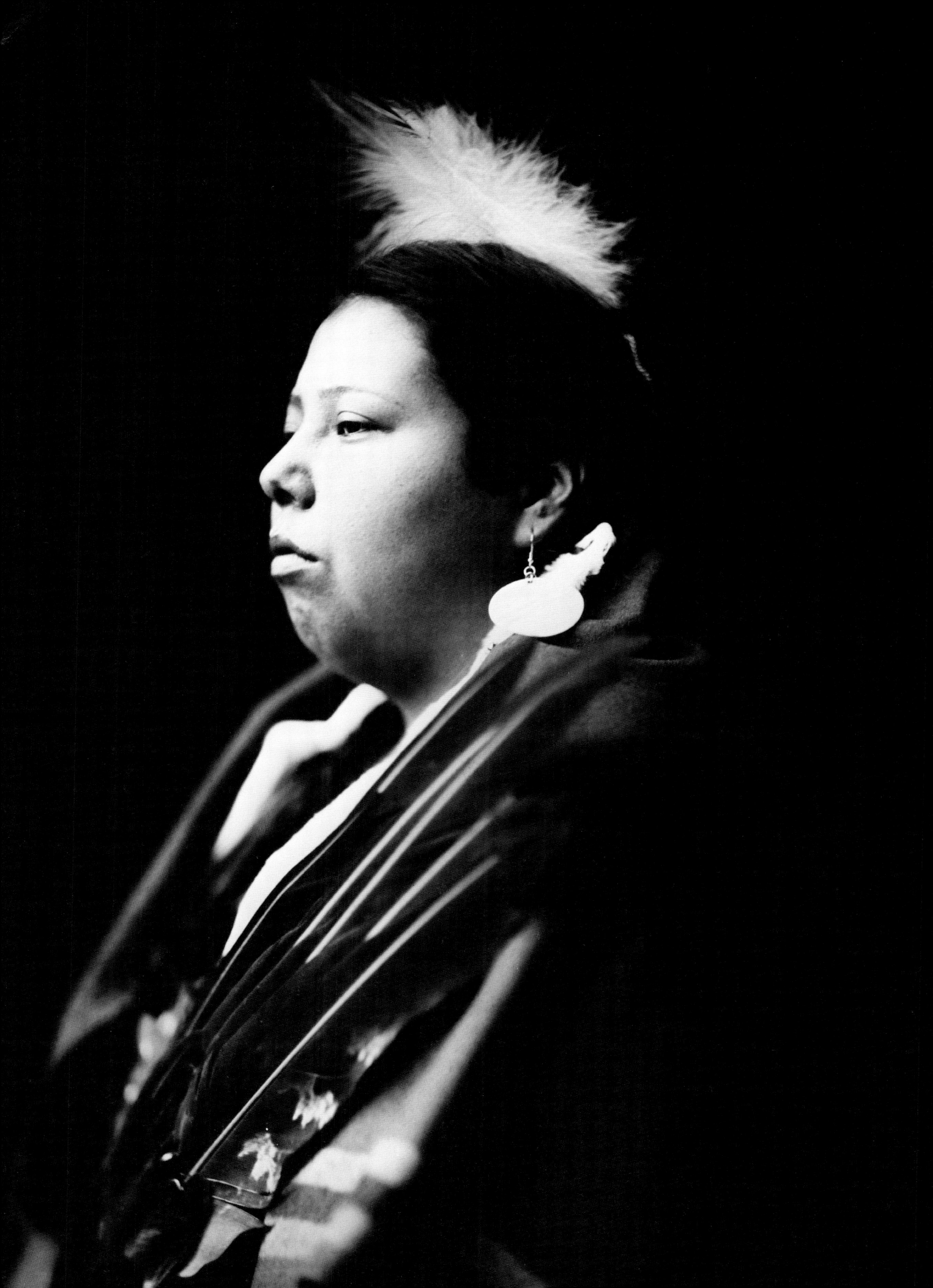

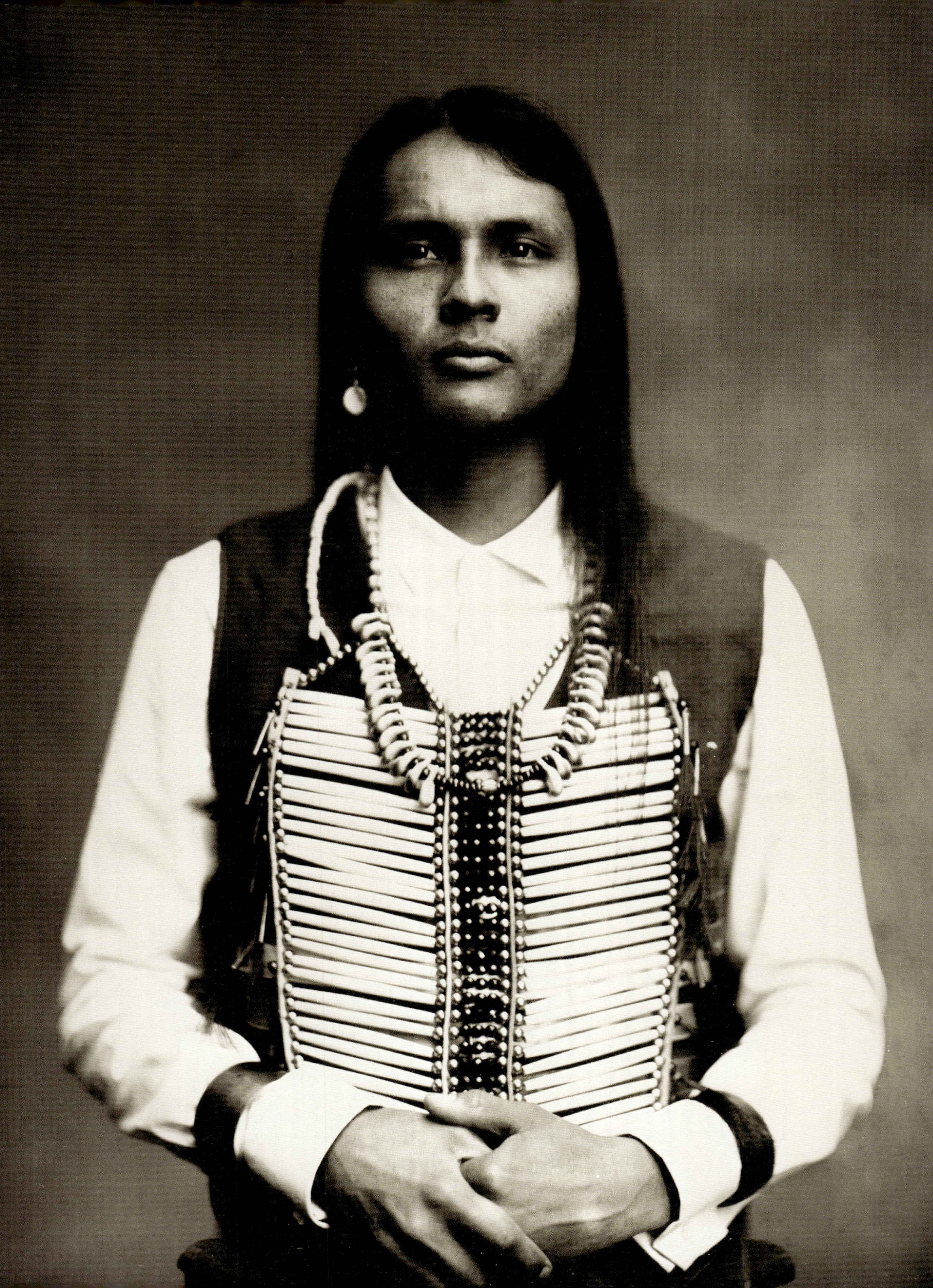

"Travels Alone" *Gavyn Taylor Spotted Tail* | Rosebud Sioux | 7 April 2023 | Plate No. 4618

"Gator" *Tsulasgi James Lone Wolf* | Cherokee | 19 May 2023 | Plate No. 4667

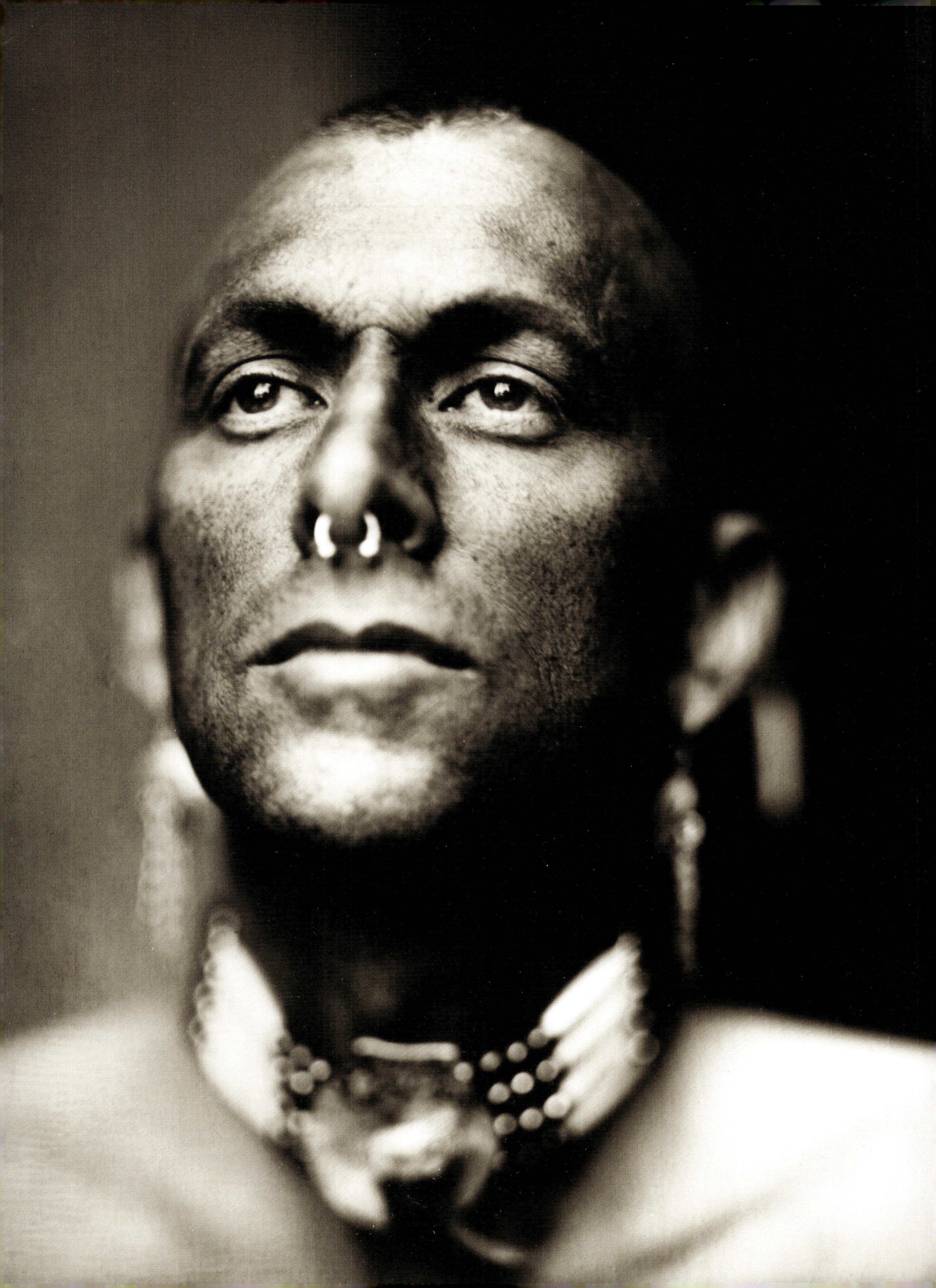

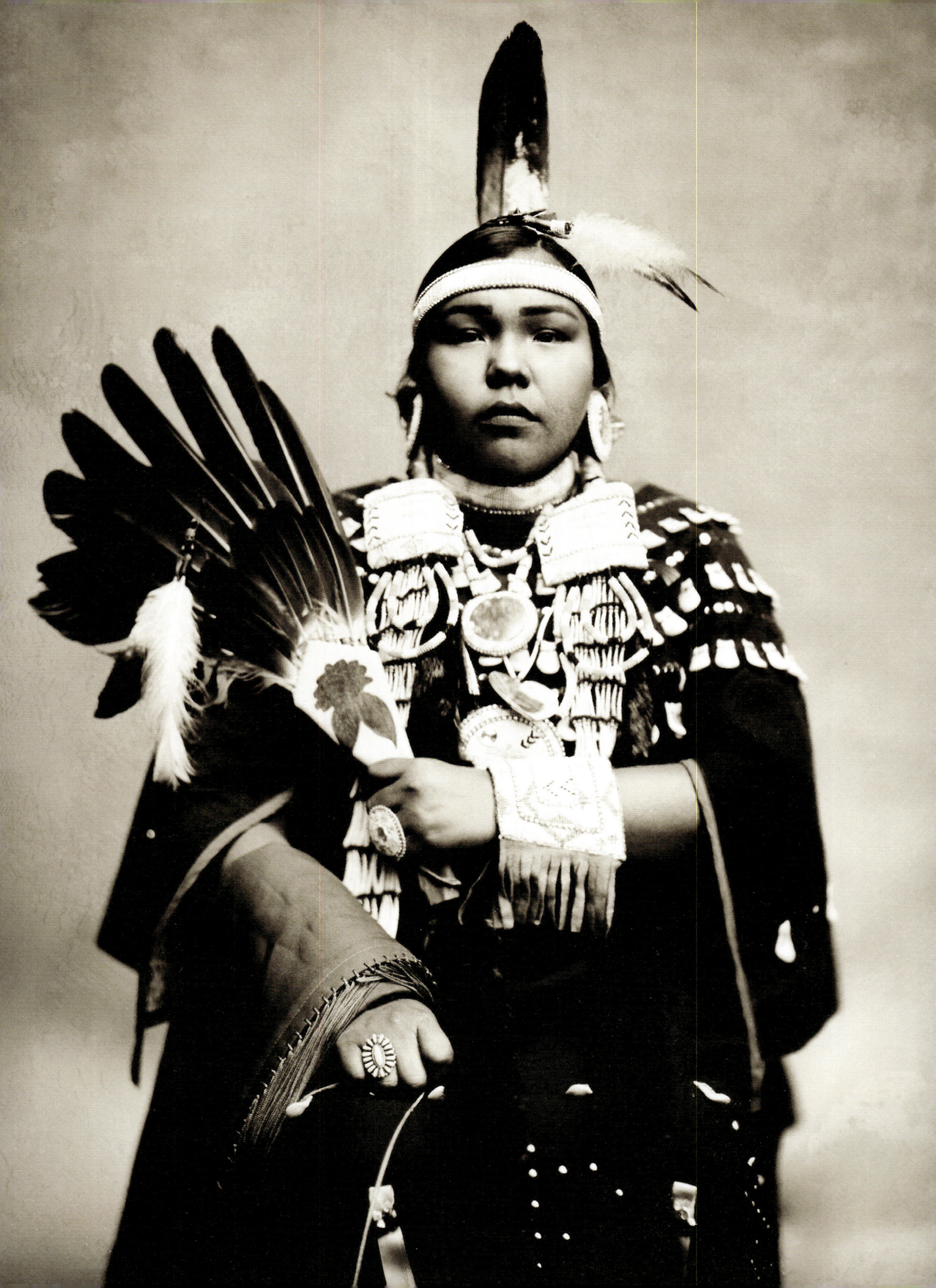

"Standing With A Strong Heart Woman" *Hannah Wreylin Roubideaux* | Rosebud Lakota Sioux / Crow Creek Dakota Sioux | 22 September 2023 | Plate No. 4808

“Osprey Hawk” *Donald Eugene Iceman, IV* | Fort Peck Sioux / Dakota | 23 June 2023 | Plate No. 4706

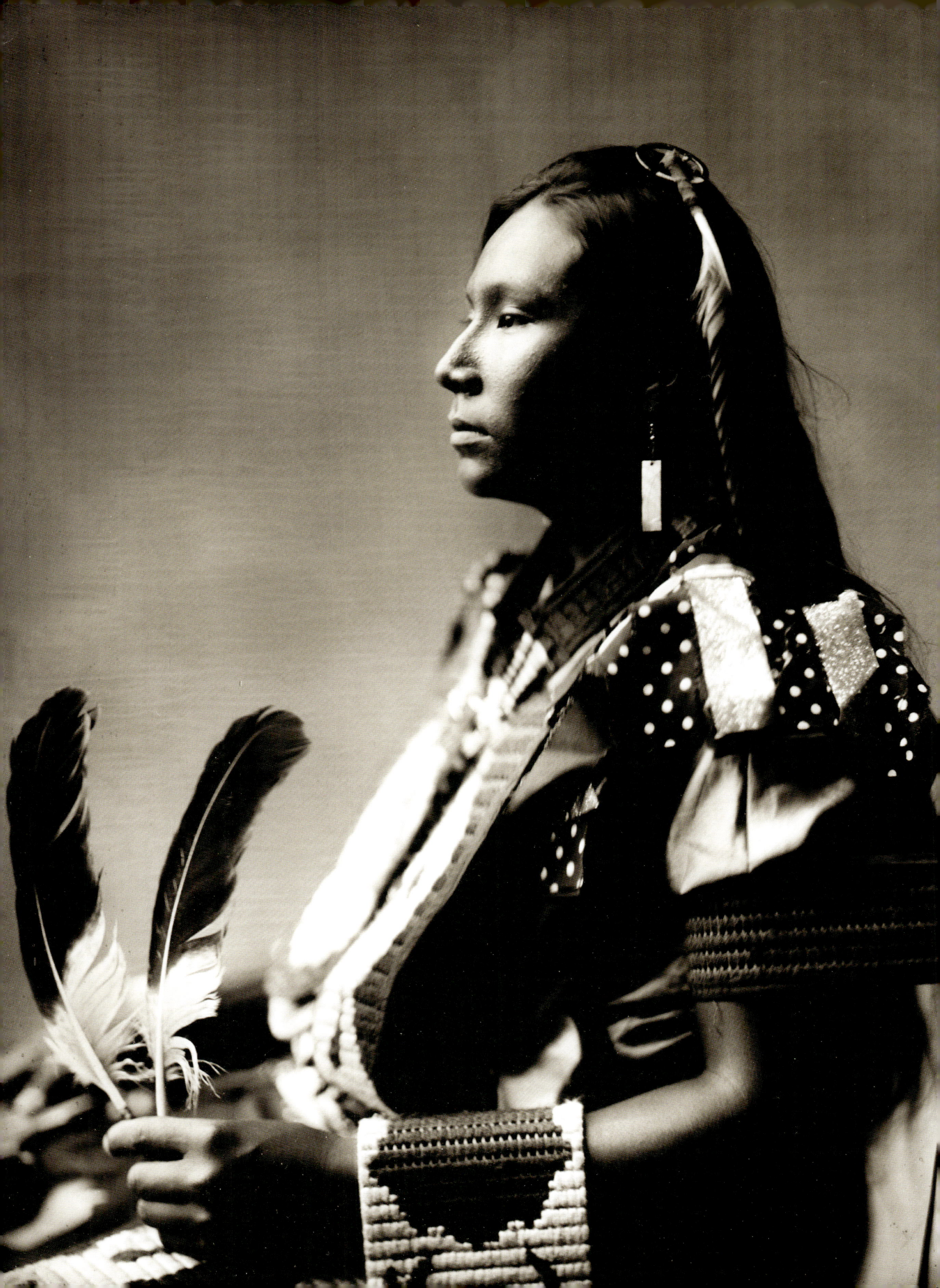

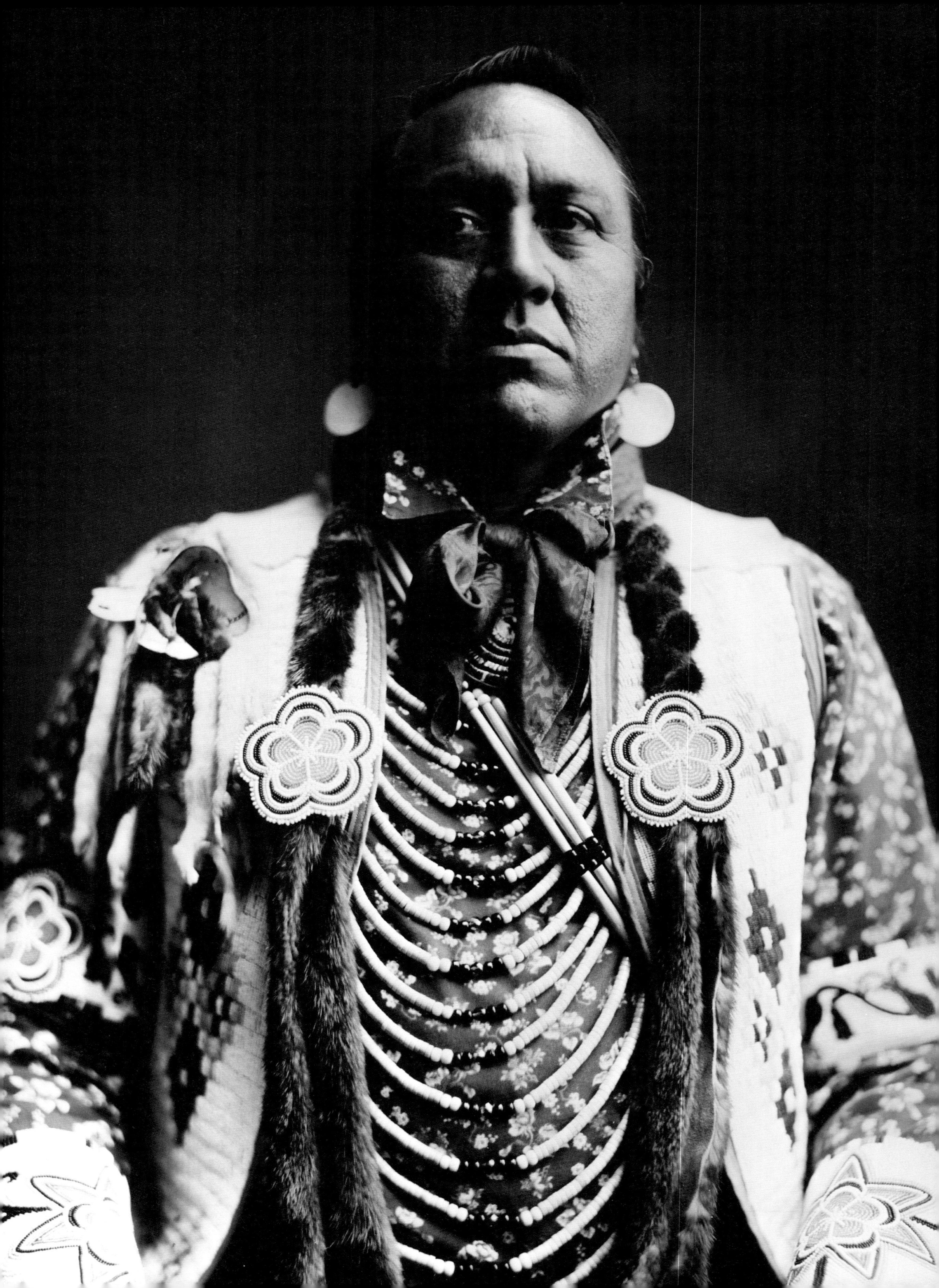

"The Sun Rays" *Shandin Hashkeh Pete* | Salish / Navajo | 23 July 2021 | Plate No. 3968

"The War Hero" *Kelvin Louis Grant* | Omaha Tribe of Nebraska | 10 September 2021 | Plate No. 4014

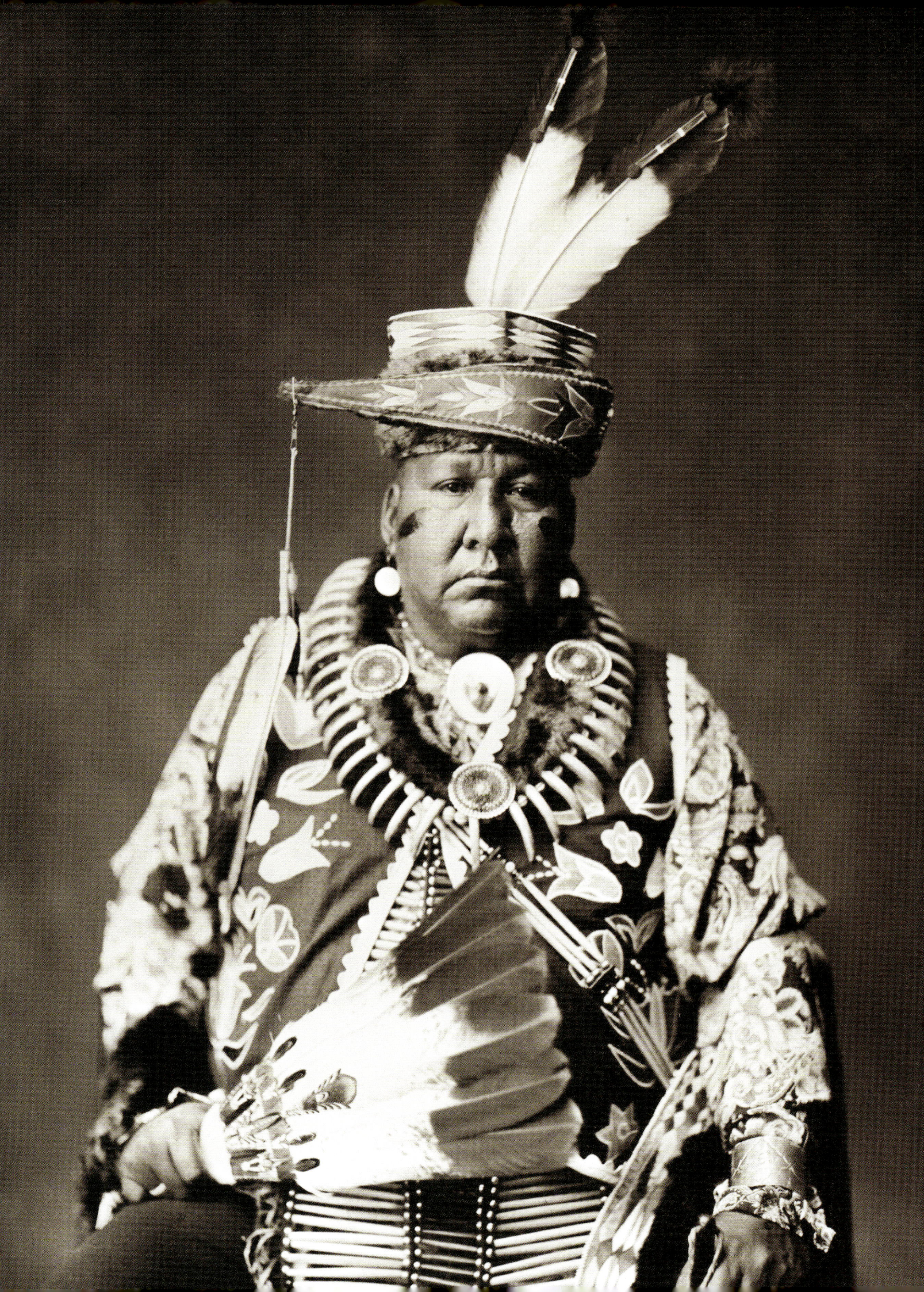

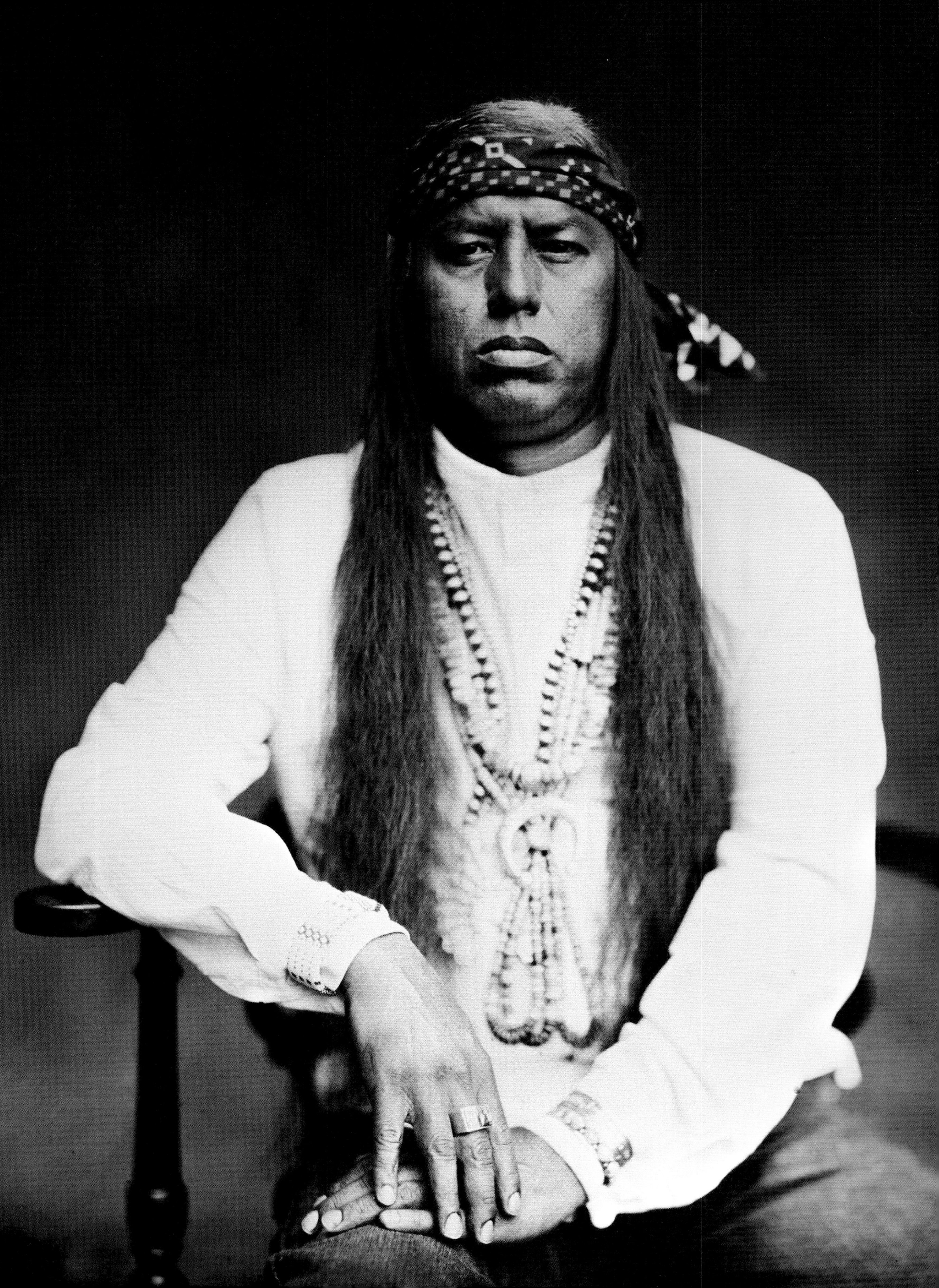

"Whistling Eagle" *Shawn Goodluck* | Dine | 9 September 2022 | Plate No. 4382

"Woman Who Stands Strong" *Tatianna Faith Wright* | Pejutazizi / Sisseton Wahpeton | 7 April 2023 | Plate No. 4623

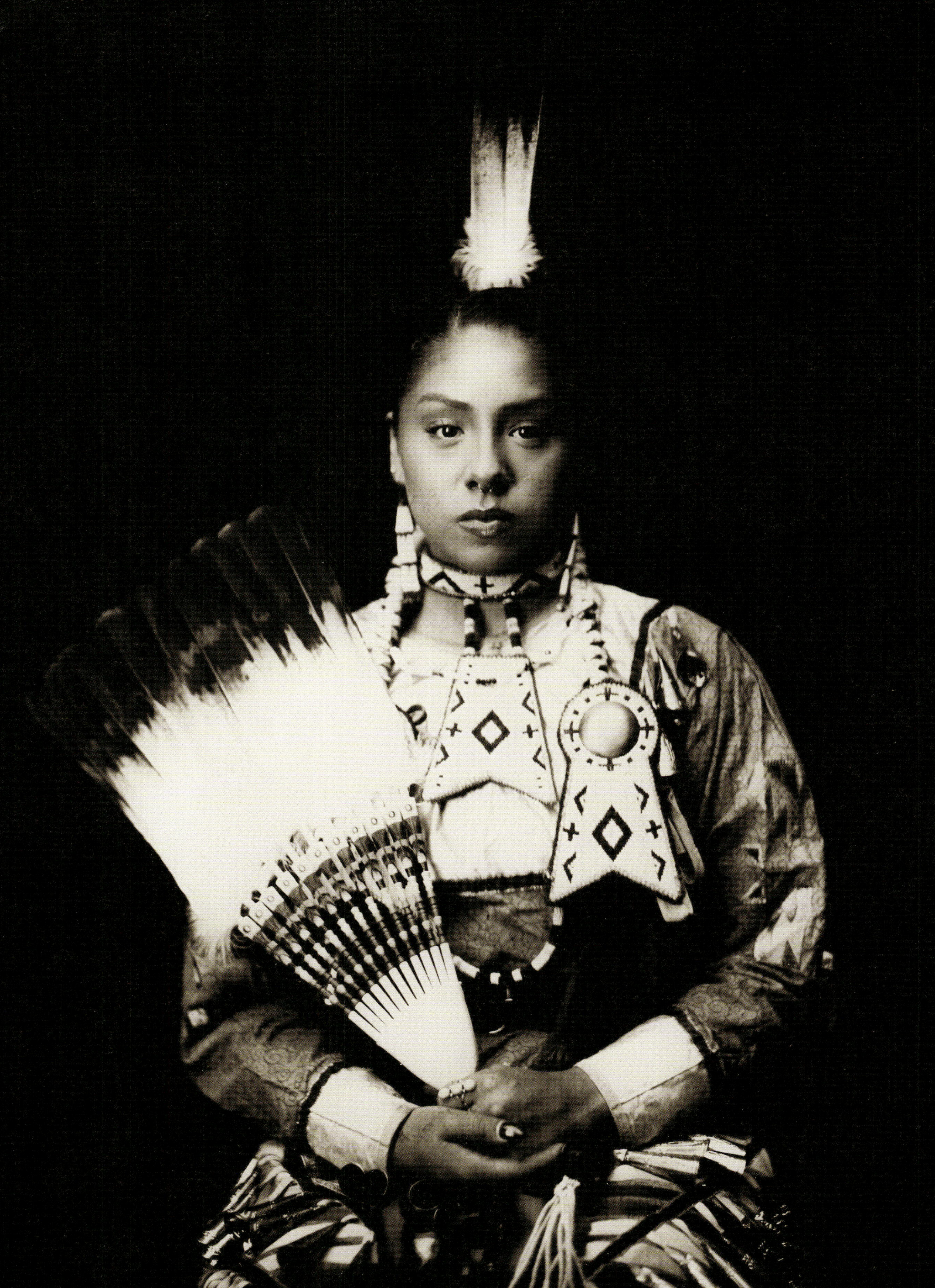

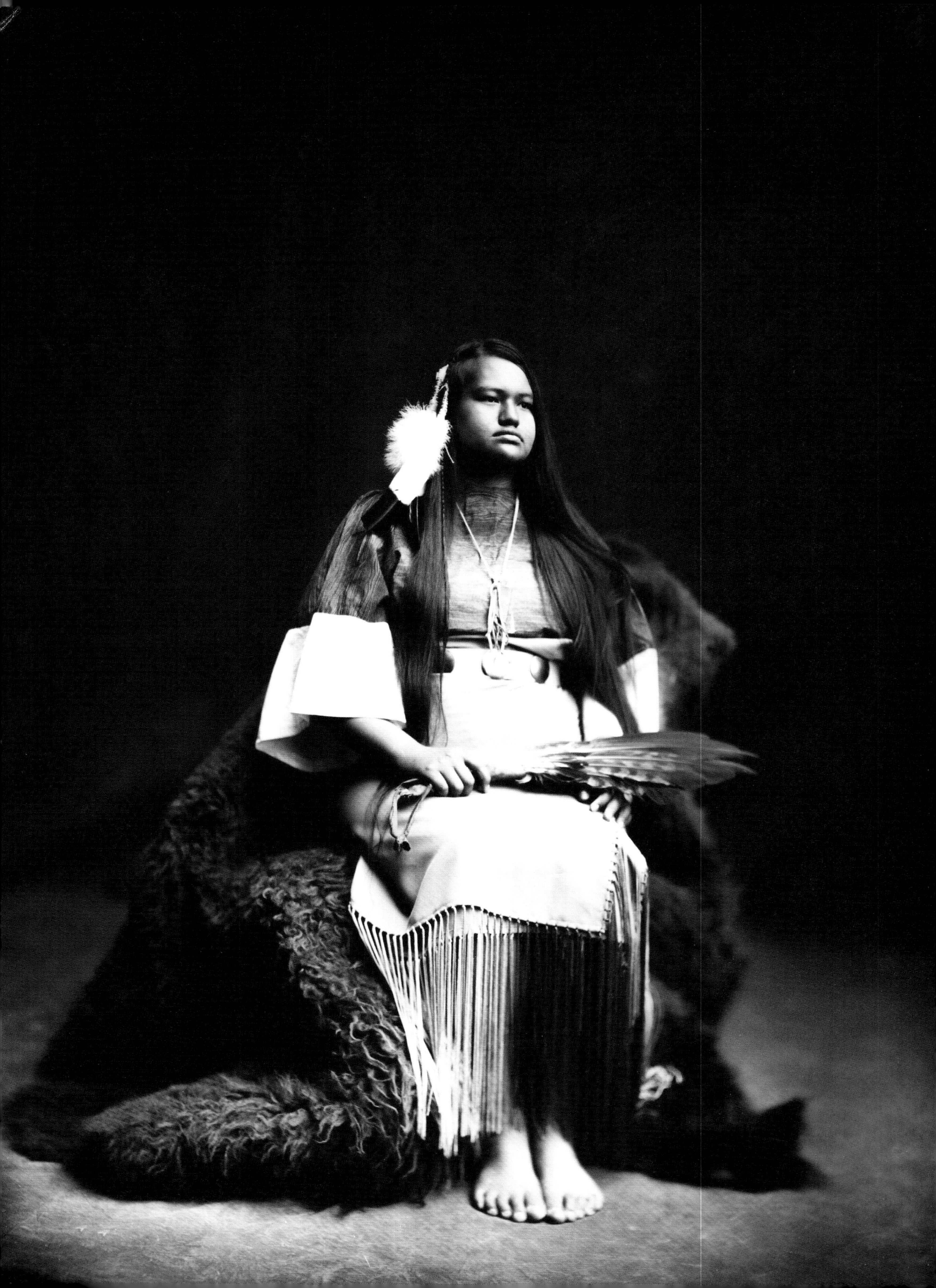

“Running Buffalo” *Zahiyah Cash Negonsott* | Lakota / Kickapoo | 20 May 2022 | Plate No. 4269

“Eagle Soaring Upwards” *Maddox Rain Eagle* | Cheyenne River Sioux | 4 August 2023 | Plate No. 4753

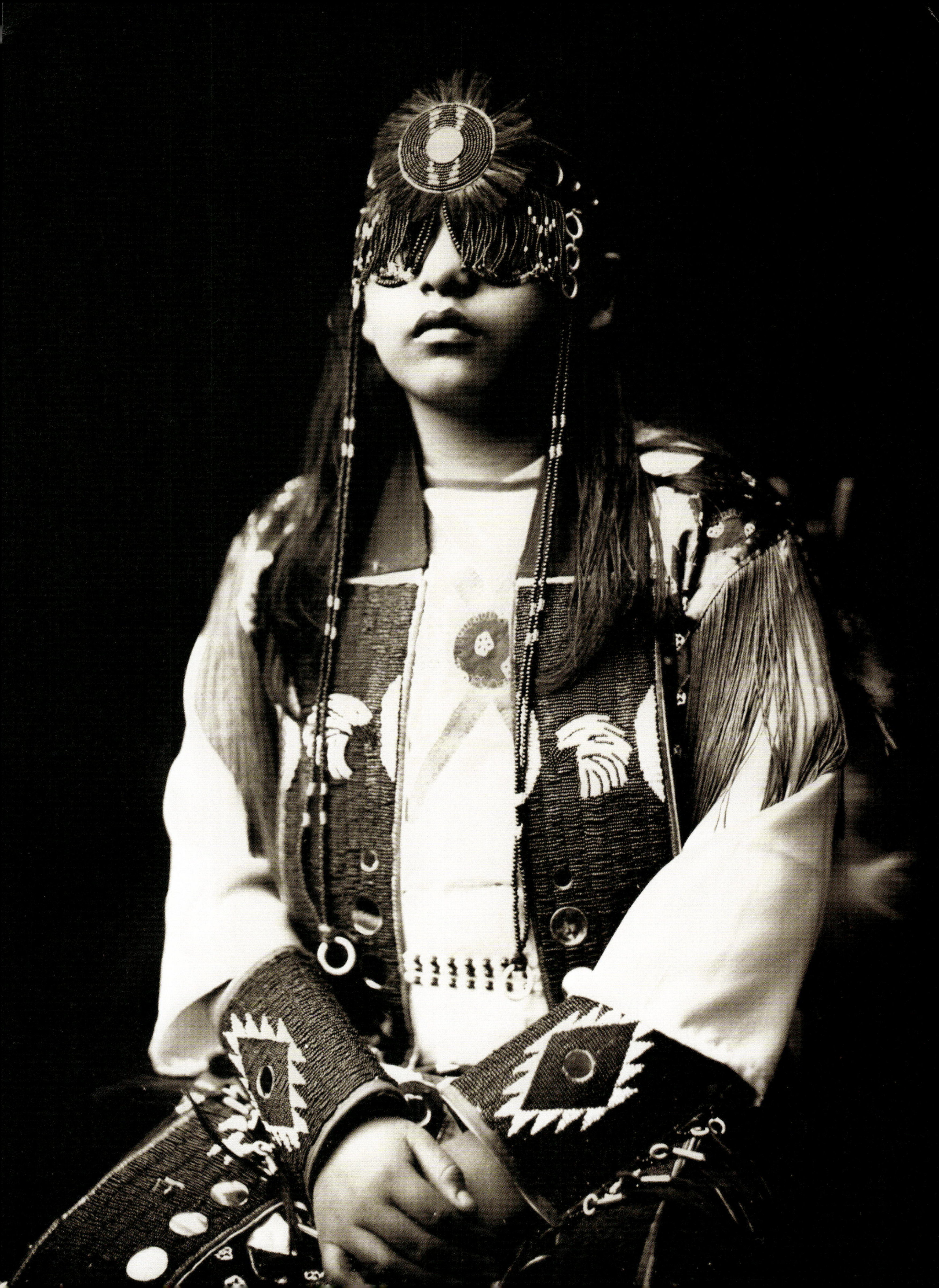

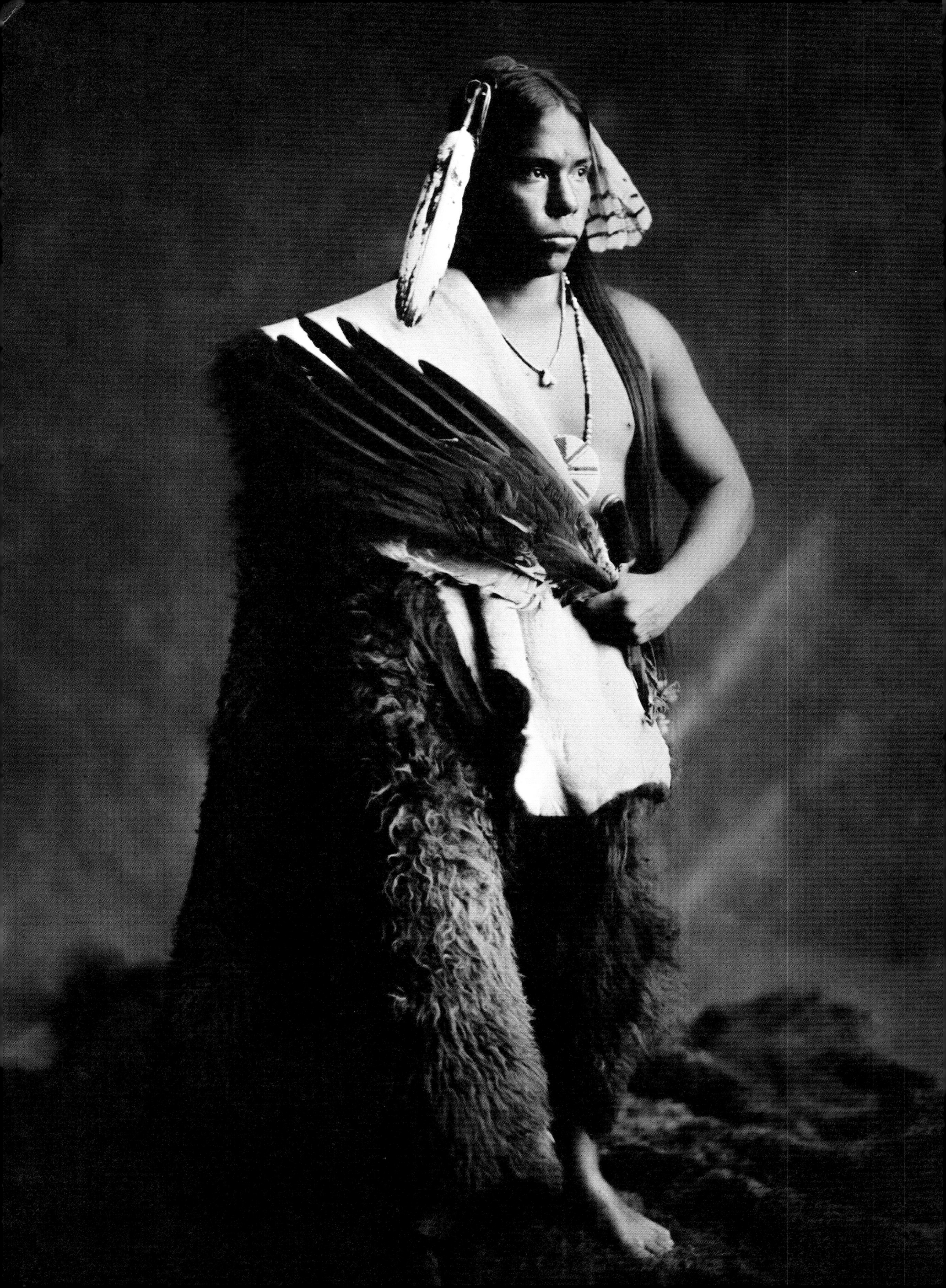

"Four Bulls" *Dion Taylor Bolman* | Hidatsa / Mandan / Arikara / Hunkpapa | 2 September 2022 | Plate No. 4375

Index

The Third 250 Native Americans Photographed

Northern Plains Native American / A Modern Wet Plate Perspective / Volume Three

Chante James Lambert **Pg. 56**	***"Bear Heart"***	*Spirit Lake Dakota Nation*	**#4450**	**11/4/22**
Charley Alana Little Eagle	***"Blue Eyes Woman"***	*Fort Peck Assiniboine Sioux*	**#4631**	**4/14/23**
Charlie Nicole Cuny	***"Red Hawk Woman"***	*Oglala Lakota*	**#4540**	**1/27/23**
Chaske Little Bear	***"Little Bear"***	*Standing Rock Sioux*	**#4543**	**2/3/23**
Cheryl Jane Funmaker	***"The Lightning Reveals Itself"***	*Ho-Chunk / Standing Rock Sioux*	**#4024**	**9/10/21**
Cheryle Danielle Good Bird	***"Uses Cedar In Ceremonies Woman"***	*Mandan / Hidatsa*	**#4046**	**10/8/21**
Cindy Marie Farlee	***"Song Bird Woman"***	*Cheyenne River Sioux*	**#4704**	**6/23/23**
Clay Flying Eagle LaRocque **Pg. 40**	***"Red Elk Whistling"***	*Turtle Mountain Pembina Chippewa*	**#4022**	**9/10/21**
Collin Tru Hale	***"Buffalo Looking"***	*Mandan / Hidatsa / Mescalero Apache / Dine*	**#4118**	**1/7/22**
Connie Lea Baker	***"Red Cloud"***	*Turtle Mountain Band of Chippewa*	**#4585**	**3/10/23**
Connie Lynn Filesteel	***"Good Woman"***	*Aaniih / Nakoda*	**#4161**	**2/11/22**
Conwin Eldrick Blake Iceman	***"Redtail Hawk"***	*Fort Peck Sioux / Dakota*	**#4705**	**6/23/23**
Cordell Todd Mann	***"Iron Eyes"***	*Hidatsa*	**#4795**	**9/15/23**
Corey Lee Davis, Sr.	***"Thunderbird Warrior"***	*Turtle Mountain Band of Chippewa*	**#4264**	**5/20/22**
Corey Lee Davis, Jr **Pg. 31**.	***"Talking Raven"***	*Hunkpapa Sioux / Turtle Mountain Band of Chippewa*	**#4266**	**5/20/22**
Councilwoman Victoria Judith Brugh	***"Woman Goes Out"***	*Mandan / Arikara*	**#3975**	**8/6/21**
Cree Rayah Sage Delorme **Pg. 20**	***"Thunderbird Woman Calling From Afar"***	*Cree / Ojibwe / Dakota*	**#4682**	**6/2/23**
Dakotah Rae Jourdain **Pg. 39**	***"Red Road Woman"***	*Crow Creek Sioux Dakota / Red Lake Ojibwe*	**#4038**	**9/24/21**
Danica Victory White	***"Red Eagle Girl"***	*Arikara / Dakota*	**#4276**	**6/3/22**
Danielle Pauline SeeWalker	***"Pretty Feather Tail Woman"***	*Hunkpapa Lakota*	**#4842**	**10/13/23**
Dayla Alea Taylor **Pg. 23**	***"Taylor"***	*Isanti Dakota*	**#4501**	**12/9/22**
Deland James Davis, Jr.	***"Davis"***	*Turtle Mountain Band of Chippewa / Oglala Sioux / Hunkpapa Sioux*	**#4635**	**4/14/23**
Denise Kathryn Lajimodiere	***"White Thundercloud Woman"***	*Turtle Mountain Band of Ojibwe*	**#4520**	**1/13/23**
Dennis Allen Young Bear	***"Bear Skin"***	*Meskwaki*	**#4358**	**8/19/22**
Dennis Howling Wolf, Jr. **Pg. 47**	***"Wild Horse"***	*Mandan / Hidatsa / Arikara*	**#4525**	**1/20/23**
Denver Bryce Spotted Bear **Pg. 15**	***"Rolling Thunder"***	*Mandan / Hidatsa / Arikara*	**#4137**	**1/28/22**
Destiny Marie Big Crow	***"Sacred Red Star Woman"***	*Oglala Lakota / Navajo*	**#4396**	**9/16/22**
Destiny Shay Jundt	***"Blue Spotted Spirit Woman"***	*Sisseton Wahpeton Sioux*	**#4579**	**3/3/23**
Dion Taylor Bolman **Pg. 108**	***"Four Bulls"***	*Hidatsa / Mandan / Arikara / Hunkpapa*	**#4375**	**9/2/22**
Donald Eugene Iceman, IV **Pg. 95**	***"Osprey Hawk"***	*Fort Peck Sioux / Dakota*	**#4706**	**6/23/23**
Donna Rosha Pike	***"Walking Wind Woman"***	*Isanti*	**#4851**	**10/27/23**
Donovan Gerald Lambert	***"Bear Shield"***	*Spirit Lake Dakota Nation*	**#4452**	**11/4/22**
Doris Jane Omeasoo	***"Mother Earth"***	*Plains Cree*	**#3978**	**8/10/21**
Duane Romaine McGillis **Pg. 32**	***"Holy Man"***	*Turtle Mountain Band of Chippewa*	**#4574**	**3/3/23**
Durand Lee Hamley, III	***"Hamley"***	*Turtle Mountain Band of Chippewa / Mandan / Hidatsa / Arikara*	**#4651**	**5/5/23**
Dustin Chad Thunder Hawk	***"Thunder Hawk"***	*Standing Rock Sioux / Oglala Lakota / Turtle Mountain Band of Chippewa*	**#4142**	**1/28/22**

Ebony Reece Tiger	***"Powerful Elk Woman"***	*Yankton Sioux / Standing Rock Sioux*	**#4875**	11/17/23
Eden Rose Cavanaugh	***"Carries A Good Banner Woman"***	*Spirit Lake Dakota*	**#4311**	7/8/22
Elaina Christine Poitra	***"Standing Strong Woman"***	*Chippewa Band of Indians*	**#4352**	8/19/22
Elizabeth Rae Eagle	***"Red Shawl Woman"***	*Cheyenne River Sioux*	**#4754**	8/4/23
Elliott Curtis Ward	***"Many Deeds"***	*Standing Rock Sioux*	**#4474**	11/18/22
Eloisa Garcia Tamez, RN, PhD, FAAN	***"Tamez"***	*Lipan Apache Band of Texas*	**#4305**	7/1/22
Emily Grace Poitra	***"Red Shadow Woman"***	*Turtle Mountain Band of Chippewa*	**#4165**	2/18/22
Eyaconape Tasunka Fox	***"One Who's Good With Horses"***	*Arikara / Hidatsa / Hunkpapa Lakota*	**#4678**	5/26/23
Frances Lorraine Merz	***"Woman With A Strong Inner Voice"***	*Standing Rock Sioux*	**#4413**	10/7/22
Francisca Tobacco	***"Tobacco"***	*Lakota*	**#4272**	5/20/22
Frankie Jo Morin	***"White Buffalo"***	*Turtle Mountain Band of Ojibwe*	**#4521**	1/13/23
Gavyn Taylor Spotted Tail **Pg. 88**	***"Travels Alone"***	*Rosebud Sioux*	**#4618**	4/7/23
Gaylan George Little Eagle	***"Brave Eagle"***	*Standing Rock Hunkpapa Sioux*	**#4629**	4/14/23
Genesis Elisa Rosales **Pg. 16**	***"Shining Star From The West"***	*Turtle Mountain Ojibwe / Cora*	**#4821**	9/29/23
George Bernard Keeps Eagle	***"Keeps Eagle"***	*Standing Rock Sioux*	**#4212**	4/1/22
Gerald Anthony Jefferson **Pg. 35**	***"Bear Turns Itself Around And Makes Them Well"***	*Hidatsa / Hunkpapa*	**#4376**	9/2/22
Gerald Carty Monette	***"Early Thunder"***	*Turtle Mountain Pembina Chippewa*	**#4368**	7/29/22
Gisele Wichoni Tobacco	***"Strong Girl With Shawl"***	*Lakota / Kickapoo*	**#4270**	5/20/22
Gloria Ann Brennan	***"Flag Woman"***	*Arikara*	**#4836**	10/13/23
Gregory Seth LeBeau **Pg. 19**	***"Two Spirit"***	*Turtle Mountain Band of Chippewa / Cheyenne River Lakota Sioux*	**#4214**	4/1/22
Hannah Wreylin Roubideaux **Pg. 92**	***"Standing With A Strong Heart Woman"***	*Rosebud Lakota Sioux / Crow Creek Dakota Sioux*	**#4808**	9/22/23
Harrison Martin Young Bear	***"Young Bear"***	*Meskwaki*	**#4359**	8/19/22
Helen Cordelia Crow Ghost-Alkire	***"Woman Who Holds Herself With High Honor"***	*Standing Rock Sioux Lakota*	**#4033**	9/17/21
Hunter Gray Decoteau	***"Ocean Bear"***	*Turtle Mountain Band of Chippewa*	**#4164**	2/18/22
Irene Joyce Omeasoo	***"Bear Woman Standing In The Mountain"***	*Plains Cree*	**#3979**	8/10/21
Isabella Aiukli Cornell	***"Beauty"***	*Choctaw*	**#4323**	7/15/22
Izsak Howard Davis	***"Red Fox"***	*Turtle Mountain Band of Chippewa*	**#4267**	5/20/22
Jaimie Rose Little Bear	***"Little Bear"***	*Hunkpapa Lakota*	**#4544**	2/3/23
Jake Jimmy Tiger	***"Snake"***	*Seminole Nation*	**#4322**	7/15/22
Jake Jordan Fox **Pg. 43**	***"Thunder Wolf"***	*MHA Nation / Standing Rock Sioux*	**#4697**	6/9/23
Jalen Chase Atchico	***"Red Buffalo"***	*Fort Peck Sioux*	**#4707**	6/23/23
James Elden St. John **Pg. 27**	***"St. John"***	*Crow Creek Hunkpati Dakota*	**#4785**	9/8/23
James Joseph Decoteau	***"Strong Heart Man"***	*Turtle Mountain Band of Chippewa*	**#4163**	2/18/22
James Patrick Grinnell	***"Eagle Whistler"***	*Hidatsa / MHA Nation*	**#4610**	3/31/23
Janay Rose St. John	***"Has A Tail"***	*Crow Creek Sioux*	**#4838**	10/13/23
Janet Louise Alkire	***"Woman Who Holds Herself With High Honor"***	*Standing Rock Sioux Lakota - Tribal Councilwoman 2021*	**#4032**	9/17/21
Jasmin-Lalani Fejerang	***"Fejerang"***	*Cupa Clan of Umatac*	**#3993**	8/27/21
Jayli Lashaundrey Fimbres	***"Sacred Shawl Woman"***	*Mandan / Hidatsa / Arikara*	**#4573**	3/3/23
Jendaya Zhane Yellow Fat	***"Stands In The Wind Woman"***	*Standing Rock Sioux*	**#4082**	12/3/21
Jeremy Lee Laducer **Pg. 71**	***"Big Bear"***	*Turtle Mountain Band of Chippewa*	**#4648**	4/28/23

Jessica Naomi Howling Wolf	***"Alert Deer Woman"***	*Mandan / Hidatsa / Omaha*	**#4526**	**1/20/23**
Jhoni Kaye Big Crow	***"Her Dwelling Cloud Woman"***	*Navajo / Oglala Lakota*	**#4395**	**9/16/22**
Jodie Lea Wallette	***"Shell Woman"***	*Turtle Mountain Band of Ojibwe*	**#4411**	**10/7/22**
Jonnie Vera Lorraine Huerta	***"She Grows Her Medicine"***	*Fort Peck Sioux / Dakota*	**#4709**	**6/23/23**
Judge Andrew Lester Laverdure	***"White Buffalo"***	*Turtle Mountain Band of Chippewa*	**#4621**	**4/7/23**
Julianna Nichole Arellano	***"Sweet Grass"***	*Mandan / Hidatsa / Arikara*	**#4476**	**11/18/22**
Julianne Paige Smart **Pg. 51**	***"Smart"***	*Standing Rock Sioux*	**#4415**	**10/7/22**
Julyana Rachael Dubray	***"Porcelain Face"***	*Sicangu / Oglala*	**#4771**	**8/25/23**
Kansas James Middletent	***"Crazy Bronc Rider"***	*Lakota*	**#4752**	**8/4/23**
Karin Maureen Eagle	***"Song Of The Brightest Star"***	*Oglala Lakota*	**#4389**	**9/9/22**
Karrie Allison Zephier	***"Woman Born In The Black Hills"***	*Lower Brule Sioux*	**#4787**	**9/8/23**
Katalina Tay Shearer	***"Orange Bird Woman"***	*Turtle Mountain Ojibwe / Hunkpapa Lakota*	**#4816**	**9/29/23**
Kateri Lulyala Murphy	***"Murphy"***	*Standing Rock Sioux*	**#4160**	**2/11/22**
Kaylee Corral Hall	***"Hall"***	*Sioux / Mandan / Arikara / Hidatsa*	**#3938**	**7/2/21**
Kelene Annette Deer	***"Deer"***	*Delaware / Otoe / Navajo*	**#4011**	**9/3/21**
Kelli Rae Roberts	***"Borrows From Her"***	*Cheyenne River Sioux*	**#4755**	**8/4/23**
Kelvin Louis Grant **Pg. 99**	***"The War Hero"***	*Omaha Tribe of Nebraska*	**#4014**	**9/10/21**
Kenley Crista Hamley	***"Hamley"***	*Turtle Mountain Band of Chippewa / Mandan / Hidatsa / Arikara*	**#4652**	**5/5/23**
Kenneth Elroy Funmaker, Jr.	***"Big Bear"***	*Ho-Chunk / Meskwaki*	**#4025**	**9/10/21**
Kiya Kay-Lynn Bruno **Pg. 28**	***"Bruno"***	*Cree First Nation from Samson Cree Nation*	**#4304**	**7/1/22**
Kiera Antonique Fox	***"Winter Breeze"***	*MHA Nation / Turtle Mountain Band of Ojibwe / Southern Cheyenne / Nakoda*	**#4519**	**1/13/23**
Kimberly Sue LaRonge	***"Edge Of The Sky Woman"***	*Lac Courte Orellies Band of Ojibwe*	**#4027**	**9/17/21**
Kody Joyce Murphy	***"Good Teacher Woman"***	*Standing Rock Sioux*	**#4279**	**6/3/22**
Kristopher George White, Sr.	***"Hits The Bear"***	*Spirit Lake Dakota Sioux*	**#4789**	**9/8/23**
Kylie Lynn Hunts-In-Winter	***"Brave Woman"***	*Standing Rock Sioux*	**#3949**	**7/9/21**
LacyJay Redwing	***"Returns Woman"***	*Sisseton Wahpeton Oyate*	**#4594**	**3/17/23**
Lael MacKenzie Middletent	***"Good Voice Woman"***	*Lower Brule Sioux*	**#4751**	**8/4/23**
Laila Ann Marie Murphy	***"Murphy"***	*Standing Rock Sioux*	**#4159**	**2/11/22**
Laleeyah Lita Aguilera	***"Red Woman"***	*Crow Creek Sioux*	**#4840**	**10/13/23**
Larry Eugene Fasthorse	***"Bear Cloud"***	*Standing Rock Sioux*	**#4703**	**6/23/23**
Laura Ann Schad	***"Schad"***	*Cheyenee River Lakota*	**#4004**	**9/3/21**
Laureen Rose Omeasoo	***"Omeasoo"***	*Plains Cree*	**#3980**	**8/10/21**
Lilly Chene Rose Dixon **Pg. 52**	***"Evergreen"***	*Hidatsa / Isleta Laguna Pueblo / Cochiti*	**#4431**	**10/14/22**
Lindalee Bruner	***"Northstar"***	*Anishinabe Ojibwe Chippewa*	**#4759**	**8/18/23**
Lisa Ranae Miller	***"Miller"***	*Ihanktowan Sioux*	**#3940**	**7/2/21**
Lluvia Jazlene Uribe-Kitto	***"Bright Woman"***	*Isanti Sioux / Yankton Sioux*	**#4185**	**3/11/22**
Lonna LaRae Peters	***"Talks For Herself"***	*Nez Perce / Yakama*	**#4377**	**9/2/22**
Loretta Mae DeLong, EdD **Pg. 55**	***"Cedar Roots Woman"***	*Turtle Mountain Pembina Chippewa*	**#4340**	**7/29/22**
Lovelee Joy Holy Bull **Pg. 60**	***"Pretty Voice Crane Woman"***	*Spirit Lake Dakota / Cheyenne River Sioux*	**#4634**	**4/14/23**
Luke Gregory Baker	***"Walks In A Good Way"***	*Turtle Mountain Band of Chippewa*	**#4584**	**3/10/23**

Lyda Jade Spotted Bear	***"Eagle Woman"***	*Mandan / Hidatsa / Arikara / Dakota Sioux*	**#4136**	1/28/22
Mabahi Thayden Arthur Baker	***"Singer"***	*Mandan / Hidatsa*	**#4138**	1/28/22
Maddox Rain Eagle **Pg. 107**	***"Eagle Soaring Upwards"***	*Cheyenne River Sioux*	**#4753**	8/4/23
Maka Akan Najin Black Elk - Great Great Great Grandson of Black Elk	***"Prancing Ram"***	*Oglala Lakota*	**#4042**	10/6/21
Marcus Dominick Levings **Pg. 63**	***"White Headed Eagle"***	*Mandan / Hidatsa / Arikara / Sioux / Yakama*	**#4364**	8/26/22
Margaret Judy Kakenowash Azure	***"Blue Sky Striped Cloud Woman"***	*Turtle Mountain Band of Chippewa*	**#4016**	9/10/21
Marilyn Rose Keeps Eagle	***"Keeps Eagle Woman"***	*Standing Rock Sioux*	**#4213**	4/1/22
Marilyn Susan Peters	***"One Who Does Not Smile"***	*Nez Perce / Yakama*	**#4374**	9/2/22
Mathew Adrian Foolish Bear	***"Two Hearts"***	*Mandan / Hidatsa / Arikara*	**#4882**	12/1/23
Matthew Steven Schanandore	***"Schanandore"***	*Mandan / Hidatsa / Oneida*	**#4103**	12/17/21
Mayo James Pena	***"Blue Warrior"***	*Standing Rock Sioux / Gila River Hopi*	**#4234**	4/22/22
Megan Denise White Bear	***"Ree Woman"***	*MHA Nation / Arikara*	**#4730**	7/28/23
Melanie Ann Minafore	***"Flag Woman"***	*Arikara*	**#4826**	10/6/23
Melanie Jo Baker	***"Blue Star Woman"***	*Standing Rock Sioux*	**#4835**	10/13/23
Michael Crandall Bissonette - Great Grandson of Chief Stabber and Chief Little Wound **Pg. 64**	***"Walks With Spotted Eagle Feather"***	*Oglala Sioux*	**#4230**	4/22/22
Michael Paul Faith - Great Great Grandson of Miles Crazy Walking	***"Buffalo Soldier"***	*Standing Rock Sioux - Chairman of Standing Rock Sioux (2017-2021)*	**#4070**	11/12/21
Miko Star Brule	***"Brule"***	*Apache / Aztec*	**#4708**	6/23/23
Mimikwas Kalika Mae Acikahte	***"Butterfly Rosebud"***	*Cowessess First Nation / Assiniboine / Saulteaux*	**#4748**	8/4/23
Misty Blue Young Bear, RN **Pg. 76**	***"Bayokia"***	*Meskwaki / Omaha*	**#4357**	8/19/22
Monica Martha Dixon	***"Circle Around The Sun"***	*Isleta Laguna Pueblo / Cochiti*	**#4430**	10/14/22
Morning-Glory Omeasoo	***"Eagle Woman"***	*Samson Cree*	**#3981**	8/10/21
Moses James Lambert	***"American Horse"***	*Hunkpapa Sioux / Oglala Sioux / Arikara*	**#4556**	2/10/23
Myah Jade Red Horse	***"Helps Amongst The People"***	*Cheyenne River Sioux*	**#4619**	4/7/23
Naida Medicine Crow	***"Searching For Relatives Woman"***	*Crow Creek Hunkpati Dakota*	**#4010**	9/3/21
Nakeezaka Suloostu Jack	***"Breaks The Belt"***	*Shoshone Bannock / Dine*	**#3966**	7/23/21
Nakoosa Stara Moreland	***"Where The Three Rivers Meet"***	*The Confederated Tribes of Grand Ronde*	**#3972**	7/23/21
Naomi Lillian Cross **Pg. 67**	***"Loves By The Stars Woman"***	*Hunkpapa / Oglala*	**#4827**	10/6/23
Ndaanis Bineeshi Ikwe Herman	***"Litle Bird Woman"***	*Turtle Mountain Band of Chippewa*	**#4632**	4/14/23
Nicole Rose Gipp	***"Gipp"***	*Standing Rock Sioux*	**#4295**	6/17/22
Noah Ree Fox	***"Roaming Wolf"***	*Arikara / Turtle Mountain Band of Ojibwe*	**#4523**	1/13/23
Oketwsha Roberts	***"Snow"***	*Choctaw Nation of Oklahoma*	**#3953**	7/16/21
Okoye Xavier Young Bear	***"Friend"***	*Meskwaki*	**#4356**	8/19/22
Oliver Thomas Roan Ramsey	***"Speaks With His Mind Boy"***	*Standing Rock Sioux*	**#4037**	9/24/21
Owaissa Evelyn Thelen	***"Blue Sky Woman"***	*Lac Courte Orellies Band of Ojibwe / Forest County Potawatomi*	**#4029**	9/17/21
Patricia Charlene Dixon	***"Otter Comes Out"***	*Hidatsa / Isleta Laguna / Cochiti*	**#4429**	10/14/22
Rayanne Annette Wise Spirit	***"Wise Spirit"***	*Standing Rock Sioux*	**#4475**	11/18/22
Redsky Starr **Pg. 72**	***"Sacred Bear"***	*Mandan / Hidatsa / Arikara / Yankton Sioux*	**#4387**	9/9/22

Reid Allen Walker	***"Bird Bear"***	*Mandan / Hidatsa*	**#4073**	11/19/21
Rika Daisy Lee Powaukee **Pg. 80**	***"Happiness Bringer Of Joy"***	*Nez Perce*	**#3991**	8/20/21
Ronald Dale Brugh	***"War Pony"***	*Mandan / Hidatsa*	**#3939**	7/2/21
Salisha Anne Old Bull	***"Prays With Her Water"***	*Salish / Crow*	**#3967**	7/23/21
Sallie Maurine Thurman	***"Greystone"***	*Standing Rock Sioux*	**#4782**	9/1/23
Sandra Gail Berlin	***"Star Woman"***	*Anishinaabe / Dakota*	**#4175**	3/4/22
Sashay Shyan Schettler	***"Owl Woman"***	*Nueta / Hidatsa*	**#4336**	7/29/22
Seneca Jade Skunk **Pg. 84**	***"Fighter Survivor Woman"***	*Lower Brule Sioux / Lakota*	**#4750**	8/4/23
Shanda Lynn Poitra	***"Corn Silk Woman"***	*Turtle Mountain Band of Chippewa*	**#4167**	2/18/22
Shandin Hashkeh Pete **Pg. 96**	***"The Sun Rays"***	*Salish / Navajo*	**#3968**	7/23/21
Shania Mary RedOwl	***"Woman With A Loving Heart"***	*Insati Dakota*	**#4604**	3/24/23
Shawn Goodluck **Pg. 100**	***"Whistling Eagle"***	*Dine*	**#4382**	9/9/22
Shawna Brooke Lambert	***"Looking For Eagle Woman"***	*Hunkpati Dakota / Sicangu Dakota*	**#4784**	9/8/23
Shawntay Rosemary Iron Horse **Pg. 75**	***"People Depends On Her"***	*Oglala Lakota*	**#4015**	9/10/21
Shaydi Summer Falcon	***"Dancing Butterfly"***	*Turtle Mountain Band of Chippewa*	**#4449**	11/4/22
Shelly Ward	***"Red Buffalo Woman"***	*Standing Rock Sioux*	**#4473**	11/18/22
Shilo Ann Comeau	***"Honors Mother Earth Woman"***	*Hunkapa / Turtle Mountain Band of Ojibwe*	**#4828**	10/6/23
Sidney Ahuaiti Hineaka Nehua-Jackson	***"Nehua-Jackson"***	*Maori of New Zealand*	**#4306**	7/1/22
Sidney Jo Bechtold **Pg. 48**	***"Yellow Fox Woman"***	*Rosebud Sioux*	**#4472**	11/18/22
Siliye Tiznahbah Pete **Pg. 79**	***"White Ermine"***	*Bitter Root Salish / Navajo / Klamath*	**#4146**	2/4/22
Sinte-Ska Roberts	***"White Tail"***	*Choctaw Nation of Oklahoma*	**#3952**	7/16/21
Skyla Rae Temens	***"Hummingbird In The Clear Sky"***	*Nez Perce / Yakama / Navajo*	**#4376**	9/2/22
Snowbird Rodriguez **Pg. 83**	***"Snow Bird"***	*Yaqui Yoeme / Apache*	**#4005**	9/3/21
Sonia Jade Annis	***"Annis"***	*Lakota*	**#4510**	1/6/23
Sonja Alaynee Snider	***"Good Day Woman"***	*Standing Rock Sioux*	**#4100**	12/17/21
Sonya Rae Davis	***"Giving Woman"***	*Turtle Mountain Band of Chippewa*	**#4265**	5/20/22
Summitt Sahara Baker	***"Guides Woman"***	*Nueta / Hidatsa*	**#4335**	7/29/22
Susan Ann Halsey	***"Halsey"***	*Standing Rock Sioux*	**#3948**	7/9/21
Susseli Nizhoni Pete	***"Baby Bear"***	*Bitter Root Salish / Navajo / Klamath*	**#4147**	2/4/22
Sydnee Rae Davis	***"Blue Bird"***	*Turtle Mountain Band of Chippewa*	**#4263**	5/20/22
Syer Saige-Migiziins Laducer	***"Little Medicine Eagle"***	*Turtle Mountain Band of Chippewa*	**#4649**	4/28/23
Sylvia Julia Joanna Bissonette **Pg. 87**	***"Early Light Woman"***	*Oglala / Grand Traverse Chippewa*	**#4435**	10/21/22
Tatianna Faith Wright **Pg. 103**	***"Woman Who Stands Strong"***	*Pejutazizi / Sisseton Wahpeton*	**#4623**	4/7/23
Taylor Jordan Schad, Esq.	***"Schad"***	*Cheyenne River Lakota*	**#4008**	9/3/21
Teagan Rae Decoteau	***"Little Drum"***	*Turtle Mountain Band of Chippewa*	**#4293**	6/17/22
Thaine Keaton Thunder Hawk	***"Crow Ghost"***	*Oglala Lakota / Hunkpapa Sioux*	**#4141**	1/28/22
Thomas Jerel Grace, Sr.	***"Brave Man"***	*Arikara*	**#4837**	10/13/23
Thomas William Red Bird	***"Lone Man"***	*Cheyenne River Sioux*	**#4406**	9/30/22
Tiana Tashina Howling Wolf	***"Lucky Day Woman"***	*Mandan / Hidatsa / Arikara*	**#4535**	1/27/23
Timothy Hunts-In-Winter	***"Hunts In Winter"***	*Standing Rock Sioux*	**#3947**	7/9/21
Tobias Lee Two Crow, SFC	***"Loud Voice"***	*Mandan / Hidatsa / Arikara*	**#4310**	7/8/22
Todd Justin Howling Wolf	***"Howling Wolf"***	*Mandan / Hidatsa / Arikara*	**#4536**	1/27/23
Travis Charles Thelen	***"Little Feather"***	*Forest County Potawatomi*	**#4031**	9/17/21

Trinity Faith Dixon	***"Dixon"***	*Hidatsa / Isleta Laguna Pueblo / Cochiti*	**#4427**	10/14/22
Trista Jade Azure	***"Azure"***	*Turtle Mountain Band of Chippewa*	**#4166**	2/18/22
Tsulasgi James Lone Wolf **Pg. 91**	***"Gator"***	*Cherokee*	**#4667**	5/19/23
Tusweca Win	***"Dragonfly Woman"***	*Cheyenne River Sioux / Oglala Sioux*	**#4595**	3/17/23
Twila Marie White Bull	***"Good Woman"***	*Hunkpapa / Oglala / Mni Coujou*	**#4548**	2/3/23
Tyeshia Jayne Natewa Ty Sparvier	***"One Feather Woman"***	*Cree / Ojibwe / Pueblo Zuni*	**#4749**	8/4/23
Vita Marie Graham	***"Woman Standing In The Back"***	*Turtle Mountain Band of Ojibwe*	**#4412**	10/7/22
Wambdi Wakiyan Clairmont	***"Leader Of The People Boy"***	*Lakota / Dakota / Ojibwe / Meskwaki / Taos Pueblo*	**#4683**	6/2/23
Wanda Jean Water	***"Walks For Them"***	*Oglala Sioux*	**#4173**	3/4/22
Wiley Joe LaRocque	***"Cloud Chief"***	*Turtle Mountain Pembina Chippewa*	**#4023**	9/10/21
Wioweste Olowan Cook and Florentine Bridget Black Spotted Horse	***"Love Song"***	*Cheyenne River Sioux*	**#4414**	10/7/22
Yanabah Eagle Horse Fox	***"Eagle Horse"***	*Arikara / Mandan / Hidatsa / Navajo*	**#4446**	10/28/22
Yolanda Marie Aguilera	***"She Who Talks To The Little People"***	*Crow Creek Sioux*	**#4841**	10/13/23
Zachary Hunter McLaughlin	***"Standing Thunder Cloud"***	*Arikara / Lakota*	**#4084**	12/3/21
Zahiyah Cash Negonsott **Pg. 104**	***"Running Buffalo"***	*Lakota / Kickapoo*	**#4269**	5/20/22
Zailey Gail Gartner	***"Sacred Elk Bone Whistle Woman"***	*Anishinaabe / Dakota*	**#4171**	3/4/22

"*Northern Plains Native Americans: A Modern Wet Plate Perspective*" series is curated by the State Historical Society of North Dakota.

For information contact the North Dakota State Archives.

Shane Balkowitsch

First and foremost I must once again thank every Native American who has ever trusted my camera and chemistry in capturing their likeness. Obviously without their belief in the goal, this series would never exist.

I also want to thank my loving family Bonnie, Abby, Greyson, Alyvia and Mahliya. They have seen first hand the work and dedication that was needed to get us this far. I recently sold my online business after 25 years and am now retired. Everything I have done up to this point was compressed into creating only one day a week. Now I will have more free time and I am excited for the future. I feel so very fortunate to be on this path and truly believe in my heart this is why I have been put here on Earth.

I want to thank Chelsy Ciavarella for once again designing this book. Her eye for detail is amazing and I am grateful to her for being committed to this series of books. I also want to acknowledge Alessandro Gibellini, my German camera maker. He custom made Red Molly I and II, my studio cameras that I used to make these plates. I also need to thank Dana Sullivan of Bostick and Sullivan, the purveyor of the wet plate chemistry that I have used since day one.

I have been asked many times if I will stop taking Native American portraits once I reach my goal of 1000 plates. The simple answer is NO. This is my life's work and I will continue to honor my friends for as long as I can.

Shane Bart Balkowitsch "Shadow Catcher" Maa'isda tehxixi Agu'agshi – Hidatsa
Nostalgic Glass Wet Plate Studio, Bismarck, North Dakota

What is Life? "It is the flash of a firefly in the night. It is the breath of a buffalo in the wintertime. It is the little shadow which runs across the grass and loses itself in the sunset. The True Peace. The first peace, which is the most important, is that which comes within the souls of people when they realize their relationship, their oneness, with the universe and all its powers, and when they realize that at the center of the universe dwells Wakan-Taka (the Great Spirit), and that this center is really everywhere, it is within each of us. This is the real peace, and the others are but reflections of this. The second peace is that which is made between two individuals, and the third is that which is made between two nations. But above all you should understand that there can never be peace between nations until there is known that true peace, which, as I have often said, is within the souls of men.

”

Nicholas Black Elk

Oglala Sious & Spiritual Leader (1863-1950)

Northern Plains Native Americans: *A Modern Wet Plate Perspective*

Archives Curating Original Black Glass Ambrotypes

1. **State Historical Society of North Dakota**, North Dakota Heritage Center, *612 E. Boulevard Ave., Bismarck, North Dakota (Primary Archive Possessing All Official Plates for the Series)*
2. **Photomuse**, The Museum of Photography, *Thrissur District, Kerala, India*
3. **The Heard Museum**, 2301 N. *Central Ave., Phoenix, Arizona*
4. **MHA Nation**, *404 Frontage Rd., New Town, North Dakota*
5. **Colorado Springs Pioneers Museum**, *215 S. Tejon St., Colorado Springs, Colorado*
6. **Arikara Cultural Center**, *100 Sahnich Dr., Roseglen, North Dakota*
7. **The University of New Mexico's Center for Southwest Research and Special Collections (CSWR)**, Zimmerman Library, *1st Floor, 1900 Roma Ave. N.E., Albuquerque, New Mexico*
8. **South Dakota State Historical Society**, *900 Governors Dr., Pierre, South Dakota*
9. **The Rourke Art Gallery + Museum**, *521 Main Ave., Moorehead, Minnesota*
10. **Gabriel Dumont Institute**, *917 22nd St. West, Saskatoon, SK S7MOR9, Canada*
11. **Tribal Historic Preservation Office**, *12554 BIA Highway 711, Agency Village, South Dakota*
12. **Minnesota Historical Society**, *345 W. Kellogg Blvd., Saint Paul, Minnesota*
13. **State Historical Society of Iowa**, *600 E. Locust St., Des Moines, Iowa*
14. **Musee d'Archeologie Nationale**, *Chateau, Place Charles de Gaulle, 78100 Saint-Germain-en-Laye, France*
15. **The Plains Art Museum**, *704 1st Ave. N, Fargo, North Dakota*
16. **Oklahoma Historical Society**, *800 Nazih Zuhdi Dr., Oklahoma City, Oklahoma*
17. **Pitt Rivers Museum**, University of Oxford, *South Parks Road, Oxford OX1 3PP, United Kingdom*
18. **Wisconsin Historical Society**, *816 State St., Madison, Wisconsin*
19. **California State Library**, California History Section, *900 "N" Street, Sacramento, California*
20. **Musee Cantonal d'Archeologie et d'Histoire**, *Palais de Rumine, Place de la Riponne 6, CH-1005 Lausanne, Switzerland*
21. **Florida Historical Society**, Library of Florida History, *435 Brevard Ave., Cocoa, Florida*
22. **State Archives of Florida**, *500 S. Bronough St., Tallahassee, Florida*
23. **Washington State Historical Society**, Washington State History Research Center, *1911 Pacific Ave., Tacoma, Washington*
24. **Prairie Village Museum**, *102 Highway 2 S.E., Suite A, Rugby, North Dakota*
25. **Lyman Allyn Art Museum**, *625 Williams St., New London, Connecticut*
26. **Nebraska State Historical Society**, *1500 "R" Street, Lincoln, Nebraska*
27. **Montana Historical Society**, *225 N. Roberts, P.O. Box 201201, Helena, Montana*
28. **Confederated Tribes of Grand Ronde – Chachalu Museum & Cultural Center**, *9615 Grand Ronde Rd., Grand Ronde, Oregon*
29. **Arizona Historical Society – Library, Archives and Collections,** *1300 N. College Ave., Tempe, Arizona*
30. **Meskwaki Cultural Center and Museum,** *303 Meskwaki Rd., Tama, Iowa*

31. **State Historical Society of Iowa,** Iowa Department of Cultural Affairs, *402 Iowa Ave., Iowa City, IA 52240*
32. **Sitting Bull College,** Library, *9299 Highway 24, Fort Yates, ND 58538*
33. **Museum of Indigenous People** (formerly Smokie Museum), *147 N. Arizona Ave., Prescott, AZ 86301*
34. **Dahl Arts Center** (Rapid City Arts Council) *713 7th St., Rapid City, SD 57701*
35. **The Flanigan Anthropological Library,** *3357 South, 525 West, Bountiful, UT 84010*
36. **Karl May Museum,** *Karl-May-Strabe 5, 01445 Radebeul, Germany*
37. **Taube Museum of Art,** *2 N. Main St., Minot, ND 58703*
38. **Camera Museum,** *369 Macon St., McDonough, GA 30253*
39. **Dickinson Museum Center** (Joachim Reginal Museum), *188 Museum Dr. E., Dickinson, ND 58601*
40. **Idaho State Historical Society** (Idaho State Archives), *2205 Old Penitentiary Rd., Boise, ID 83712*
41. **Booth Western Art Museum** (Smithsonian Affiliate), *501 N. Museum Dr., Cartersville, GA 30120*
42. **The James Museum of Western & Wildlife Art,** *150 Central Ave., St. Petersburg, FL 33701*
43. **New Mexico History Museum,** *113 Lincoln Ave., Santa Fe, NM 87501*
44. **State Archives of Michigan,** *702 W. Kalamazoo St., Lansing, MI 48915*
45. **Staatliche Museen zu Berlin,** *Arnimallee 27, D-14195, Berlin, Germany*
46. **Mid-American All-Indian Museum,** *650 N. Seneca, Wichita, KS 67203*
47. **The Field Museum of Natural History,** *1400 S. Lake Shore Dr., Chicago, IL 60605*
48. **Museum of the Great Plains,** *601 N.W. Ferris Ave., Lawton, OK 73507*
49. **Lake Region Public Library** (Devils Lake), *423 7th St. N.E., Devils Lake, ND 58301*
50. **Aurora University Schingoethe Center,** *1315 Prairie St., Aurora, IL 60506*
51. **The Charleston Museum,** *360 Meeting St., Charleston, SC 29403*
52. **Oregon Historical Society,** *1200 S.W. Park Ave., Portland, OR 97205*
53. **St. Mary Sister Archive,** Mother House, *P.O. Box 2576, Bismarck, ND 58502*
54. **H.H. Bennett Studio and Museum,** *215 Broadway Ave., Wisconsin Dells, WI 53965*
55. **National Museums Scotland,** Chambers Street, Edinburgh, *EH1 1JF, Scotland*
56. **The National Museums of World Culture,** *Sodra Vagen 54, 402 27 Goteborg, Sweden*

A Note About The Series

This book is volume three in the series of four that will be published. It represents a careful selection of 50 of my favorite images from plates 500-750. When I reach the milestone of 1000 plates another selection of 50 images will comprise the final fourth volume in the series.

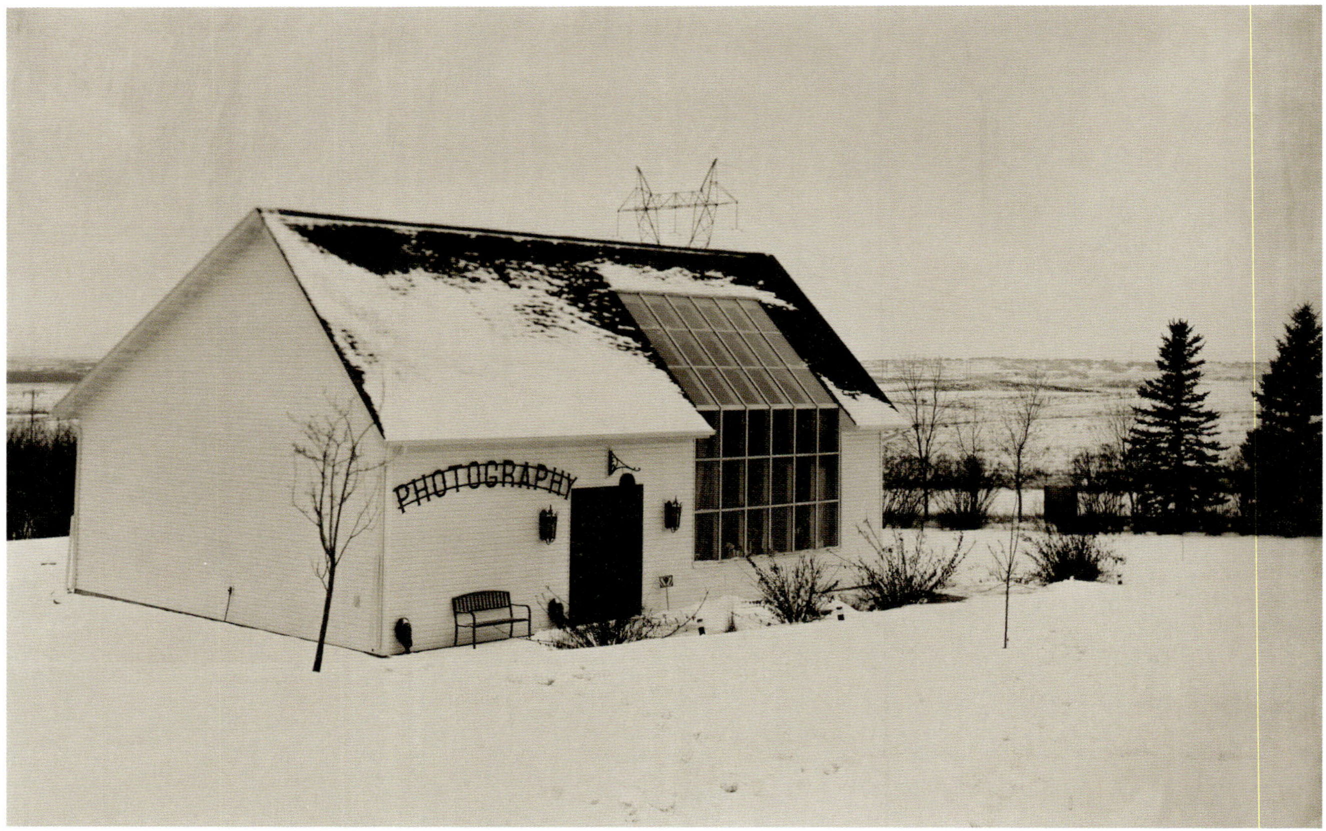

"Winter At Nostalgic Glass" by Shane Balkowitsch taken on March 29th, 2024, his 5000th plate since Oct. 4th, 2012

Colophon

First edition, 2024

Library of Congress Cataloging-in-Publication data is available from the publisher.

Hardcover edition
ISBN: 978-1-943876-63-1
Printed and bound in Latvia

Graphic Design and Layout by Chelsy Ciavarella
Proofreading by Emily Kubischta

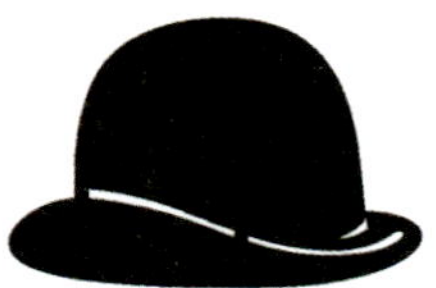

Published in 2024 by
Shane Balkowitsch
Nostalgic Glass Wet Plate Studio
2703 Big Sky Circle
Bismarck, ND 58503

shane@balkowitsch.com
www.nostalgicglasswetplatestudio.com

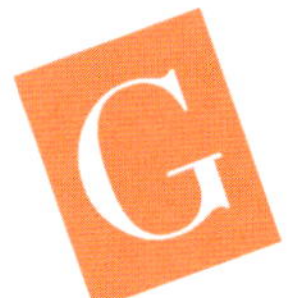

Distributed by
G Editions
500 Seventh Avenue
8th Floor
New York, NY 10018

www.geditions.com
media@geditions.com